Our Choices, Our Lives

*Caitlyn —
Here's to strong
women with
Irish name.
Kathleen george Kearney*

*10/10/02
Caitlin,
Thanks for supporting choice.
Yours in solidarity,
Krista Jacob*

Our Choices, Our Lives

Unapologetic Writings on Abortion

Edited by Krista Jacob

Writers Advantage
San Jose New York Lincoln Shanghai

Our Choices, Our Lives
Unapologetic Writings on Abortion

All Rights Reserved © 2002 by Krista K. Jacob

No part of this book may be reproduced or transmitted in any form or by any means, graphic, electronic, or mechanical, including photocopying, recording, taping, or by any information storage retrieval system, without the permission in writing from the publisher.

Writers Advantage
an imprint of iUniverse, Inc.

For information address:
iUniverse, Inc.
5220 S. 16th St., Suite 200
Lincoln, NE 68512
www.iuniverse.com

Unless othewise noted, individual authors hold copyright to their material. Contributions are included with author consent for the limited purpose of creating this anthology.

ISBN: 0-595-23001-6

Printed in the United States of America

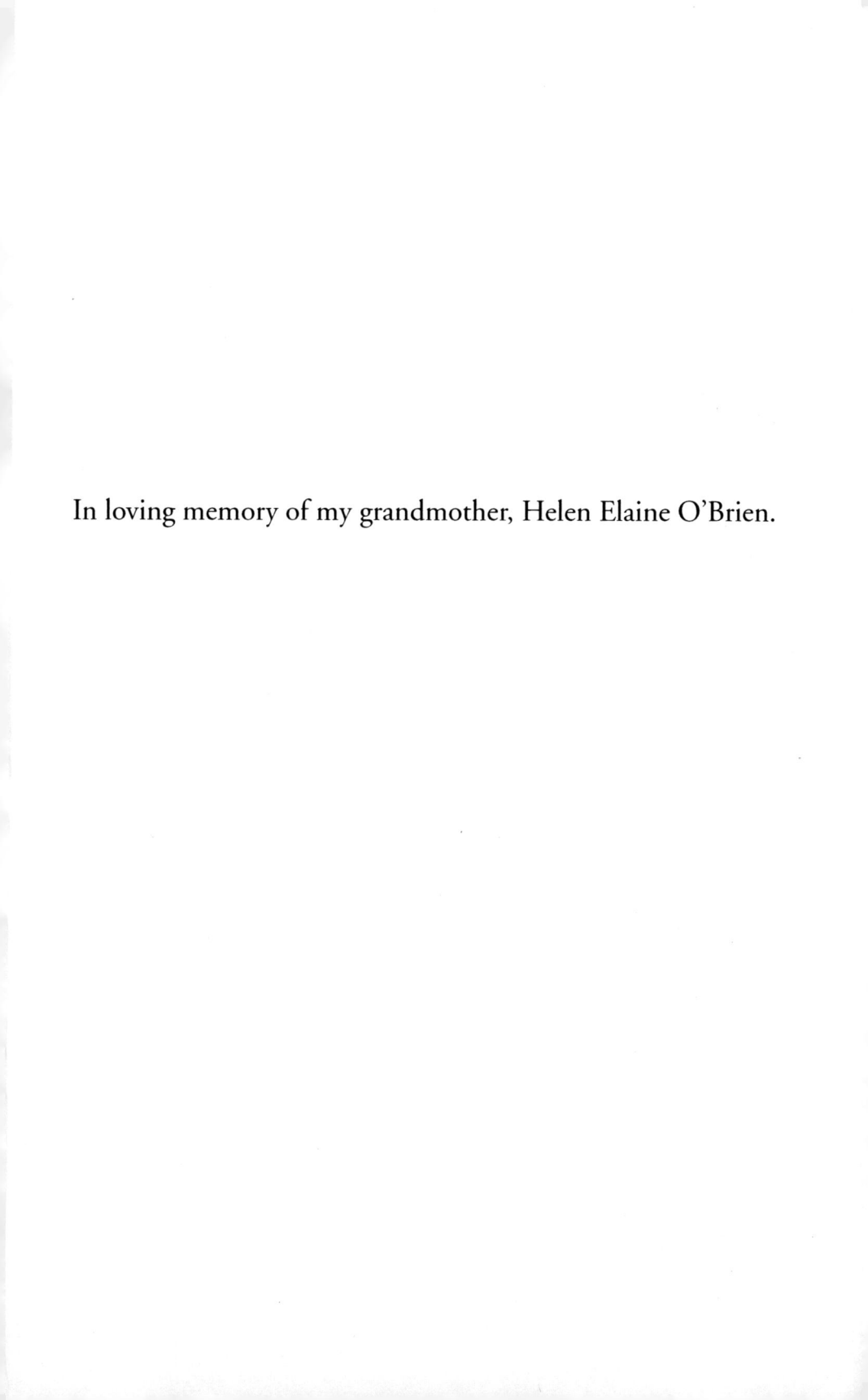

In loving memory of my grandmother, Helen Elaine O'Brien.

EPIGRAPH

Not the church, not the state, women will decide their fate.
Pro-choice slogan

No woman is required to build the world by destroying herself.
Rabbi Sofer, 19th Century

I fear for the future. I fear for the liberty and equality of the millions of women who have lived and come of age in the 16 years since Roe was decided…For today, at least, the law of abortion stands undisturbed. For today, the women of this Nation still retain the liberty to control their destinies. But the signs are evident and very ominous, and a chill wind blows.
Justice Blackmun; U.S. Supreme Court; Dissenting Opinion; Webster v. Reproductive Health Services; July 3, 1989.

Contents

List of Photographs xiii

Foreword xv
    Karen Kubby

Preface xxi

Acknowledgements xxv

List of Contributors xxvii

Introduction xxxvii
    Krista Jacob, Editor

PART I: ABORTION TESTIMONIES: BEFORE AND AFTER LEGAL ABORTION 1

    WOMEN KNOW 3
        Anne Baker and Jean Stewart Berg

BEFORE ROE V. WADE 6

    CHILDHOOD PAUSE 6
        Carol Harder

    MOTHERLODE, MOTHERLORE 11
        Kathleen George Kearney

    UNEXPECTED BLESSING 14
        Reverend Mary Beth O'Halloran

    PATTY 17
        Polly Rothstein

    INTERVIEW WITH FRAN 21
        Michelle Menter

AFTER ROE V. WADE 26

SPEAKING MY TRUTH 26
Chandra Silva

I ONLY CALL WOMEN 36
Avra

SURPRISE (OR EVERYTHING TO DO WITH HOPE) 39
Rhonda Chittenden

THOUGHTS DURING MY ABORTION 40
Kathleen George Kearney

SILENCE 43
Jennifer Powis

MULTIPLE CHOICE 45
Katherine M. DePasquale

HURRICANES AND OTHER BACKLASH 48
Kristy Beckman, age 17

TIPPED UTERUS 51
Toni Presti

THAT WAS A VERY GOOD YEAR 53
Marie King

A TRIP TO HELL (AT AGE FOURTEEN) 58
Mary Grant

MY ADULT LIFE IN SIX EASY INSTALLMENTS 78
Kathleen George Kearney

A CHOICE BETWEEN TERRIBLE AND AWFUL 86
Nicole Foster

MY STORY 92
Suzanne Seas

THE NECESSARY EVIL 104
Rochelle Moser

PART II: VOICES FROM INSIDE THE ABORTION CLINIC 109

A CLINIC VISIT 111
DeDe VanSlyke with Krista Jacob

BLESSING FOR THE ABORTIONIST'S HANDS 120
Elizabeth Moonstone

INTERVIEW WITH DR. CARRIE TERRELL 122
Rhonda Chittenden

DYSPLASIA 124
Dr. Virginia Bartholin

PAPER-CLOTHED STRANGERS 127
Jennifer New

CLINIC TESTIMONY 131
Carla Vogel

THE BREEZE IN THE WAITING ROOM 133
Jenny Higgins

WHY WE ARE SENDING YOU HOME 135
Shari Aronson

HEAT WAVE 140
Jenny Higgins

JUST ANOTHER DAY AT WORK 141
Kathleen George Kearney

I PREPARE THE FIFTEEN-YEAR-OLD 143
Jenny Higgins

DEBBIE, WHO STANDS OUTSIDE A CLINIC EVERY SATURDAY 145
Kathleen George Kearney

HONORING PLEASURE 147
Sue Schlangen

PART III: ORGANIZING FOR CHANGE: RELIGIOUS AND POLITICAL ACTIVISTS SPEAK OUT 151

    OPTING OUT OF THE ABORTION WAR: FROM THE BIRMINGHAM BOMBING TO SEPTEMBER 11TH 153
        Margaret R. Johnston

    ABORTION AND POWER: THE EFFECTS OF PATRIARCHY AND CLASS ON WOMEN'S REPRODUCTIVE OPTIONS 170
        Shaianne Osterreich

    A RADICAL LANGUAGE OF CHOICE 176
        Krista Jacob

    POSSIBILITIES VERSUS BABIES 179
        Amy Blumenshine

    MY PRO-CHOICE CREDO 184
        Kathleen George Kearney

    MIDLAND COALITION FOR CHOICE 187
        Carole Head

    DIVERSITY IN CHOICE 190
        Alice Limehouse

    ABORTION IS A CONSTITUTIONAL RIGHT 193
        Jennifer Olencheck

    FREEDOM OF RELIGION 196
        Reverend Marguerite A. Beissert

    WOMEN AS WOMBS, WOMEN AS HOLES 198
        Chris Stark

Afterword 209
    Ashley Sovereign

About the Editor 215

Notes 217

Bibliography 221

List of Photographs

Pregnancy Test 112
   DeDe Van Slyke
Blood Test 112
   DeDe Van Slyke
Ultrasound 1 113
   DeDe Van Slyke
Ultrasound 2 113
   DeDe Van Slyke
Counseling Session 1 114
   DeDe Van Slyke
Counseling Session 2 114
   DeDe Van Slyke
Counseling Session 3 115
   DeDe Van Slyke
Procedure 1 115
   DeDe Van Slyke
Procedure 2 116
   DeDe Van Slyke
Procedure 3 116
   DeDe Van Slyke
Procedure 4 117
   DeDe Van Slyke
Procedure 5 117
   DeDe Van Slyke
Procedure 6 118
   DeDe Van Slyke
Procedure 7 119
   DeDe Van Slyke

Foreword

Karen Kubby
Executive Director, Emma Goldman Clinic, Iowa City, Iowa

Our Choices, Our Lives: Unapologetic Writings on Abortion is a collection of personal testimonies by women who have sought abortion services and by providers of those services. It concludes with a focus on political issues surrounding one of the most controversial issues of our time: allowing women to control their fertility.

It is unfortunate that the last section of the book is necessary, for abortion is a personal and medical decision. Abortion is the most commonly sought-after medical procedure by women. Forty-three percent of women in the United States will have had an abortion by the time they are forty-five years old.[1] Thus, abortion should be categorized as basic health care within mainstream medicine.

In the minds of individual women, abortion is not the political decision that some make it out to be. Women don't come to clinics and proclaim they are present to participate in a political act. Nevertheless, the last section of this text is necessary and critical. For if women are ever to truly gain personal, social, and economic equity, women must be able to control their fertility.

It is because the movement against abortion has been successful at framing the issues, creating language, and even eroding legal rights of women that the common cultural understanding of abortion is based in a political context instead of through the experiences of individuals. *Our Choices, Our Lives: Unapologetic Writings on Abortion* will help us reframe these issues, gain a different model of language used to talk about abortion, and to remove the exaggerated focus from the fetus and back to where it rightly belongs—on women.

Even some pro-choice supporters will say, "This devastating choice…" or "This heart-wrenching decision…" implying that abortion is always a negative choice, a difficult one, or one of last resort. For some women it is a complex and emotional process; for others it is a shorter and more direct one. There will always be a range of emotions among individuals, but we should not assume that for every woman who chooses abortion it is a hard decision, or an amoral/immoral dilemma, or a disempowering choice. Nor should we assume it is a flippant or instantaneous decision. When providing client-centered services, we should not assume at all. Our job as health care providers is to make sure that women with unintended pregnancies have the time, information, and emotional space to make the best decision for themselves and their families. The only assumption we should make is that women are trustworthy in making these decisions.

For some women, it is the abortion process—both the decision-making and the implementation of that decision—that is the line of demarcation where they begin to take control, to set their course, to achieve clarity about their life paths. The testimonies in *Our Choices Our Lives: Unapologetic Writings on Abortion* illustrate this poignantly.

It is one thing to be pro-choice on an ideological, philosophical, or political level. It's another thing to actually provide services. The second section of this book focuses on service providers. Abortion providers work under incredibly stressful conditions. The health-care industry is under siege. The political climate surrounding abortion services magnifies this phenomenon. Add to this the security issues that surround abortion provision at each step of the process—from welcoming women into the clinic ("Please leave your purse in the car and your coat outside the door."), as they meet the letter of state laws ("I know you are over eighteen, but I need to see a picture ID."), as they escort women to the recovery room, as they take out the garbage, and even when they choose their route by which to go home after work.

Some clinics have regular protesters. This form of disagreement, when practiced through screaming, yelling, interference to clinic access and harassment of clients, providers, and clinic staff at the office and at their homes, adds another deep layer of stress. It can also create a layer of resolve and commitment to the provision of legal basic health care for women.

This resolve can return focus once again to the client, helping her trouble-shoot financial issues (many women do not have health insurance, and when they do, it may not cover abortion services), transportation, childcare issues and other life factors. Abortion service providers may even have to deal with someone disclosing that she "doesn't believe in abortion, but wants one." This type of internal conflict is one of the more difficult challenges when living out the provision of non-judgmental health care. It can be frustrating to have someone choose to obtain medical care at your facility only to have them "shut the door" on those behind them. Even more frustrating are situations where clients return to the picket line outside the facility where they have just completed their legal and safe abortions. The commitment to confidentiality prevents these individuals from being exposed.

In the face of all of this, the commitment of the organizations and clinic owners, and the individual licensed and lay health care professionals is incredible and must be honored.

We who are abortion providers connect with clients and direct service workers everyday. As a group, we should also create on-going relationships with the community. We need to model a positive and clear way of talking about our issues in empowering ways. We need to communicate frequently and clearly about current trends in the abortion issue, as well as assaults against our physicians, our buildings, our clients, and our staff. We must ask for the support and resources we need to do our work.

We should include the academic community in this communication. Providers can facilitate connections with academics to study our processes, to see feminist principles of non-judgmental and culturally competent health care being lived out daily. We can invite academicians to let our daily experiences inform their work, as we can strive to have their academic work inform service provision and feminist health care activism. I would like to see a convergence of activism, feminism, and academics, a concept I refer to as "Actifemics." We need to rectify the so-called disconnect that frequently is present between these three disciplines. Connecting these disciplines can help shape service provision for individuals, academic frameworks, and the pro-choice movement itself.

Providers also need to facilitate relationships with state and federal policy-makers. We cannot be afraid to tell our stories, to push elected officials to be more vocal on this basic health care issue, and to help them become more articulate in their struggle to maintain this basic right. In addition to advocacy and education, some of us may face the challenge to become policy-makers ourselves.

When a woman finds out that she is pregnant, whether intentionally or not, three choices are available to her: taking the pregnancy to term and raising the child, adoption, or abortion. Each choice has its tradeoffs, as does every decision. When policy-makers talk about child bearing, their approach is almost always in positive terms. When laws are passed to mandate state-provided information about a pregnant woman's choices, the content of the information speaks to the positive aspects of adoption and attempts to steer women away from abortion. Why doesn't the law allow for an account of the negative aspects of adoption or the positive aspects of abortion?

If these laws are truly about ensuring full and non-judgmental information to pregnant women, a different public policy strategy is needed. Information should be available where pregnant women first seek help—at family practice and obstetrics and gynecology offices, crisis pregnancy prevention centers, as well as abortion providers. Once a woman has an abortion appointment, it is obvious she has already made her decision. When state-mandated "information" is then presented exclusively in this context, the underlying message becomes, "You must not have thought through your decision very well, since you chose abortion. Here is some information that will help you choose correctly." This is incredibly insulting to women.

Providers do have a process for women who are ambivalent or conflicted about their decision. It is called a "referral." Under these circumstances, a woman is referred back to her support network, to professional counseling, or to herself so that she can take more time to come to a decision about which she feels confident. Since most abortions occur within the first eight weeks of pregnancy[2] time remains in the first trimester to continue the decision-making process.

Our Choices, Our Lives: Unapologetic Writings on Abortion points us toward the creation of a new way of thinking and talking about basic health care for women, including abortion services. Only when we hear women's voices can we know that they are capable of raising children, adopting out their children, and of making a moral choice to not have children, or to not have children now. Only when we trust women to make good decisions for themselves and their families will our culture and political landscape truly move toward gender equity.

Preface

Ashley Sovereign and I first began this book project in 1997. At the time, we worked as Reproductive Health Counselors at Midwest Health Center for Women, a non-profit abortion provider in Minneapolis, Minnesota. Before we joined the clinic, we had been counselors at a rape crisis center. Our professional involvement in the anti-rape movement and the pro-choice movement made sense to us since both issues are an integral part of a woman's right to control her body, her sexuality, her fertility, and therefore her destiny.

We were compelled to create an anthology about reproductive freedom because we wanted to document what we believed was a significant theoretical shift occurring in abortion politics. While we were concerned by a growing political apathy among our generation of women and men, we also felt that there was (and still is) a tremendous amount of education and activism happening around reproductive freedom that was being neglected by the mainstream media. So we circulated the following "call for submissions" which outlined our goals:

> First, we want to provide a forum for women and men to talk candidly about their experiences with abortion in order to illuminate the reality of abortion and dispel myths perpetuated by those who seek to restrict reproductive freedom. Second, we want to foster critical analysis on the current state of abortion and reproductive freedom. Third, we want to combine various perspectives within the pro-choice movement in order to present a more holistic and well-rounded view of reproductive freedom.
>
> Potential contributors include, but are not limited to:

- Women who have had abortions
- Clinic workers (counselors, sex educators, lab staff, receptionists, security workers, nurses, doctors, etc.)
- Partners, friends, and family members of women who have had abortions.
- Activists and intellectuals
- Politicians
- Policymakers

We see this as an opportunity to empower people to speak out about reproductive freedom and, at the same time, contribute to creating feminist social change in our society. We employ a feminist perspective and seek to examine issues of class, race, gender, sexuality, ability, age, and other interlocking oppressions. As feminist writers, we want to examine, within the context of this book, the myriad of influences these social factors have in shaping abortion discourse.

Our "call for submissions" provided a general vision for the book, and asked the contributors to outline which aspect(s) of this issue deserved the most attention. We wanted contributors to use the style of writing (conversational, academic, unconventional, poetic, theoretical, and so on) that best reflected their personal style and experience. Thus, the varied writing formats in our finished project symbolize the diversity of the contributors' lives and experiences.

Some people challenged us to provide a more narrow scope for the writers (which would have undoubtedly made the entire process easier). But, ultimately, we did not want to limit potential contributors, and instead hoped that the topics covered, and the experiences shared, would reflect the plurality of the pro-choice movement. We hope that *Our Choices, Our Lives: Unapologetic Writings on Abortion* can help challenge the misconception that all feminists, or pro-choice people, or women who've had abortions, think alike.

As a result of our limited time, space, and resources, we have inevitably left out valuable perspectives and experiences. Despite the areas in which we may be lacking, or the topics that we have left under-explored, my hope is that this anthology can be a catalyst for a new kind of discourse about abortion, a discourse that further challenges the pernicious effects of abortion restrictions, totalitarian religious dogma, male supremacy, state regulation of women's health care, the dangerous intersection of religion and government, and the hypocrisy of politicians who restrict welfare benefits while they chip away at abortion rights. Lastly, we hope that this book contributes to a discourse that fosters truth telling, despite messy contradictions, which might, on the surface, appear to undermine our pro-choice ideologies. Without shame, without apology, unimpeded access to safe and dignified abortion is our right.

Acknowledgements

In both process and product, editing a book is highly collaborative. Whether one receives help from friends, professional acquaintances, or family members, the role(s) they play is critical to the book's development and completion. A book of this magnitude required the collective work of many, many people. I am grateful to all who helped bring this book to fruition.

In the following pages you will read the powerful words of thirty-eight women who, in one way or another, are connected to the abortion issue, either through personal experience, political commitment, or both. I'm certain their words will stay with you, as they have with me, and will offer you new insights and perspectives. Thus, I would first like to express my deep gratitude to the contributors for coming out, so to speak, about their abortion experiences and pro-choice beliefs. In these conservative times, those of us who are pro-choice, whether we come from religious or secular perspectives, are too easily silenced by the voices against abortion. Indeed, in the current sociopolitical climate speaking out in support of abortion rights is a revolutionary act. Thank you for trusting me with a small part of this revolution.

To my supportive partner Jim Oliver whom I can never thank enough for his love and kindness, and for taking on more than his share of childcare responsibilities so that I could put this book together.

To Ashley Sovereign, who merits special acknowledgement because she helped me envision this project. Though she left her official role as co-editor in July of 2000, her editorial contributions and suggestions proved invaluable.

To my righteous friends who cheered me on, read my drafts, served as unofficial editors, and babysat my son: Melisse Gelula, Jennifer

Reynoldson, Joanna Anderson, Katie Miles, Elizabeth Wardle, Maria Reveiz, Mary Pat Rice, and Rhonda Chittenden.

To the women of my writing group: Emari Dimagiba Lavine, Lauri Wollner, Ahndi Fridell, Kathleen George Kearney, and Ashley Sovereign, for inspiring my creativity and for teaching me the importance of process over product.

To Basel Kasaby for his generosity and smart legal advice.

To my sister, Tamra, because I love her and am perpetually in awe of her as a woman and as a mother.

To Erica Beckman, Dr. Robert Filippone, Gloria Filippone, and Emari Dimagiba Lavine, for offering last minute assistance with the book cover design. I want to specifically thank Erica Beckman for using her talent as a photographer to record the diversity among women so that we can honor and celebrate these differences. Erica's photographs beautifully embrace the spirit of this anthology.

To my mentors who helped shape both my feminism and my commitment to social justice: Christie Munson, Dr. Myrtle K. Aydelotte, Diane Finnerty, Karen Kubby, Meredith Jacobson, Debbie Kuykendall, Reverend Doug Peters, Becky Westerfelt, Susan Clark, Liz Haller, Janice Griffin, Monya Choudhury, Trudy Gustafson, Janet Jacobs, Dr. Donna Langston, Dr. Steve Beuchler, Margaret (Peg) Johnston, Claire Newman, Anne Baker, Pat Sandin, and the compassionate staff at Midwest Health Center for Women. I'm honored to know people of such great talent and integrity.

My eternal gratitude to my mother, Deanna, and to my grandmothers, Helen O'Brien and Jayne Killbreath, for forging new paths before me, and for supporting me when I chose to forge my own.

And, finally, my sincere thanks to our copy editor, Lisa Proctor, whose remarkable editorial skills guided me through the final stages of completing this book.

List of Contributors

Shari Aronson is a freelance writer and theatre artist who lives in Minneapolis. She worked for five years as an abortion counselor and Spanish interpreter for the Midwest Health Center for Women in Minneapolis.

Avra (last name withheld) is a performance poet and writer. Born and raised in New York City, she has taught on three continents and holds a Ph.D. in English Literature.

Anne Baker has been Director of Counseling at The Hope Clinic for Women in Granite City, Illinois since 1976. She has counseled thousands of women prior to their abortions and researched the subject of emotional and spiritual coping after an abortion. She has authored the book *Abortion and Options Counseling: A Comprehensive Reference*, and self-help booklets on the subject of post-abortion coping for men and women. Her publications are used in training health professionals in the United States, Canada, Australia, South America, and South Africa.

Dr. Virginia Bartholin (pseudonym) is a doctor and mother of a four-year-old daughter. She is currently (and by choice) four months pregnant. Her life partner is a pro-feminist doctor who shares her passion for politics and women's issues. Together, they are learning a great deal about life through the process of parenting their spirited, precocious child. They enjoy travelling and long walks with their large, lovable St. Bernard dogs. The upcoming arrival of their second child will, in their humble opinion, make the world stop and celebrate!

Kristy Beckman is a college student in the Bay Area. She loves to stay in bed and write stories, poetry, political essays, and zines. Kristy first developed her passion for feminist activist work in high school, which is when she wrote "Hurricanes and other Backlash."

Reverend Marguerite (Peg) A. Beissert is a former journalist, Christian educator, and now a retired Presbyterian clergywoman. She is a widow with three adult children. Professionally she has been, and still is, an advocate for gays and lesbians. She has been associated with churches on both East and West coasts.

Jean Stewart Berg is a lifetime advocate for women's social justice. She received her M.A. in Theology from Eden Theological Seminary with special expertise in issues of Faith and Public Policy. She is author of several articles. Ms. Berg lives with her husband Dick on the Island Cozumel in Mexico, located just off the Yucatan Peninsula. Currently she serves as the Chair of the national Board of Directors of the Religious Coalition for Reproductive Choice.

Amy Blumenshine seeks to express a great generosity of being. At different times, she has worked as a clinical social worker, college instructor, journalist, Lutheran missionary, and community organizer. She and her family are active in their inner city church and neighborhood.

Rhonda Chittenden, MS, is a creative writer and collage artist whose career includes serving women and girls as a Reproductive Health Counselor, a sexuality educator, and an advocate for those in the juvenile justice system. Born and raised in Warren County, Iowa, she is a regular columnist for *Sexing the Political: A Journal of Third Wave Feminists on Sexuality*, located at www.sexingthepolitical.com. Ms. Chittenden currently makes her home in Minneapolis.

Katherine M. DePasquale graduated *Phi Beta Kappa* from Temple University, with a B.A. in English and a minor in Women's Studies. Her work has recently appeared in *Feminista* and in the anthology *Making the Harm Visible: Global Sexual Exploitation of Women and Girls*. Katherine lives and works in New York City.

Nicole Foster (pseudonym) is a mother of three and lives in the Midwest. She has a degree in journalism, but currently puts most of her energy into being a stay-at-home-mom. She is a frequent contributor to www.aheartbreakingchoice.com, which reaches out to families who have terminated a pregnancy after a bad prenatal diagnosis by providing resources for healing and an email listserv for grieving parents.

Mary Grant's (pseudonym) main focus in life has been assisting others in what she calls "Spirit or Soul Growth." She believes that every event in one's life is a symbolic representation of what exists within oneself and often serves as a block to achieving one's heart's desires. Through "reading" this symbolism, in life and in dreams, she assists others in removing their emotional and mental blocks in order to realize their true selves and manifest their heart's desires.

Carol Harder grew up in a military family. She left school at the age of fifteen because staying in school while pregnant was not an option. Once out of school, even if no longer pregnant, there was no going back. Today, she has two grown daughters and a granddaughter. After four years of living part-time in Europe, she is extremely happy to be home and settled in New Hampshire, where she resides with her husband of four years.

Mrs. Carole Head has been Treasurer of the Midland Coalition for Choice for several years, and is on the state board of Planned Parenthood Affiliates of Michigan. She owned and operated a large travel agency after her three adult children went off to college. She loves to play golf, travel with her husband Jim, and walk through the woods with their dogs.

Jenny Higgins has worked as a Medical Assistant and Counselor at two U.S. abortion clinics, one in New England and one in the Southeast. Her work with abortion patients remains among the most meaningful and compelling of her life experiences. A year after leaving her position as a counselor, she underwent her own abortion. Jenny is currently a doctoral candidate in Women's Studies and Public Health at Emory University.

Krista Jacob, editor, is founder and editor of the online journal *Sexing the Political: A Journal of Third Wave Feminists on Sexuality*, located at www.sexingthepolitical.com. She has a long history of involvement in women's issues, which includes working as a victim advocate for rape and domestic violence survivors for ten years, and as a Reproductive Health Counselor for four years. At present she is a writer, mother, and works as an on-call Reproductive Health Counselor.

Margaret R. Johnston is Director of Southern Tier Women's Services, located in Vestal, New York, where she has been providing abortion services since 1981. She is also President of the National Coalition of Abortion Providers. She is the editor of "Pregnant? Need help? Pregnancy Options Workbook," and is an advocate for quality pregnancy counseling.

Kathleen George Kearney was raised in Wooster, Ohio. She is a graduate of Macalester College, located in St. Paul, Minnesota, and of the United Theological Seminary of the Twin Cities. She has worked in the pro-choice movement for twelve years, including serving as Executive Director of the Minnesota Religious Coalition for Reproductive Rights. Currently she is a minister and abortion counselor.

Edited by Krista Jacob • xxxi

Marie King (pseudonym) is a paralegal who lives in the northeastern part of the United States. After four years in the army, she returned to school and received her bachelor's degree in Political Science in 2000. She is currently pursuing her master's degree in Communication and, after graduation, plans to attend law school, where she will focus on women's issues and the legal rights of children with special needs.

Karen Kubby is Executive Director of the Emma Goldman Clinic in Iowa City, Iowa. The Emma Goldman Clinic opened in 1973 and was the first feminist reproductive health care facility in the Midwest. Karen is a community activist and trainer. Previously, she served three-terms as a member of the City Council in Iowa City. Karen has made her living as a high school science teacher, politician, artist and administrator.

Alice Limehouse is the mother of a three-year-old daughter named Phoebe who is helping her through law school at Georgia State University In fact, her daughter attended a Constitutional Law class with her on the topic of Roe v. Wade. Alice says, "Our family is still just the two of us, so we are a pretty tight team. My choice to have her has led to a difficult path, but I have no regrets. I plan to pursue a legal career in the public interest, either through a government agency or a non-profit organization, and hope to raise Phoebe to be a loving, conscientious, pro-choice woman."

Michelle Menter lives with goldfish in Ithaca, New York. She teaches art to two very young people, coordinates an asset-building program for low-income people, and is the volunteer operations director of a community art gallery. She loves working, playing, laughing, and making art.

Elizabeth Moonstone (pseudonym) has been an abortion doctor since 1991, providing over 16,000 abortions to date. She lives with her partner and their three cats surrounded by gardens and trees, including a Celtic

Lunar Grove she planted in 1993. The trees are now taller than their house. She loves being an aunt and is newly a great-aunt, which she finds astonishing.

Rochelle Moser has a degree in English literature and is currently working toward a degree in nursing. She has worked at Planned Parenthood of Minnesota and South Dakota for seven years. In her spare time, she enjoys working out, belly dancing, and sharing her life with her husband and close friends. Rochelle is choosing to be childless because she is concerned about overpopulation and its effects on the environment. She plans to spend her life exploring the world, enriching her education, and cultivating exuberance in herself and those around her.

Jennifer New is a writer who lives in Iowa City with her husband Andrew and daughter Isabella Maji. Her work has appeared in *Salon*, *Teacher Magazine*, *MAMM*, and regional publications. Her first book, *Dan Eldon: The Art of Life*, was published by Chronicle Books in the fall of 2001.

After earning additional graduate degrees in counseling and in ministry, **Reverend Mary Beth O'Halloran** worked in churches for thirteen years. She continues to fulfill her vocation through spiritual direction, counseling, and teaching religious studies in a college and seminary in the Midwest. She has no children but has loved and influenced hundreds of young people as their counselor, minister, and teacher.

Jennifer Olenchek is the president of the Milwaukee chapter of the National Organization for Women and a co-founder of Women's Political Voice, an organization whose mission is to increase the representation of women in elected office. Additionally, she chairs the Milwaukee Coalition for Choice, a coalition of pro-choice organizations.

Shaianne T. Osterreich is an assistant professor in the economics department at Ithaca College. Originally from Connecticut, she received her doctorate in economics from the University of Utah. She lived in Southern Minnesota and Northeast Ohio where she taught Economics and Women's Studies while writing her dissertation. Dr. Osterreich's main research focus is on how participation in the market affects and reflects gender, race, and class-based hierarchies. Specifically, she has been working on the relationship between gendered labor markets and international trade and economic development.

Jennifer Powis and her wife Lynda, work and play in Texas. Besides going abroad on the boat, she's traveled throughout the United States enjoying the American landscape. In between hiking and climbing trips, she attends law school at The University of Texas where studying has unfortunately taken up much of her free time. She'll escape to the real world in 2003.

Toni Presti currently teaches English to speakers of other languages in New York City. She received her Master of Arts in TESOL from NYU. Her career includes acting, directing, and writing for the theatre and radio. Her essay, entitled "Tipped Uterus," was written for a collaborative performance piece directed by Jenna Freedman.

Before retiring at the end of 2001, **Polly Rothstein** headed the Westchester Coalition for Legal Abortion (NY) for thirty years. She created ProChoice IDEA: identification, education, and activation of pro-choice voters, a list made up of 70,000 pro-choice households that contain active voters. Now all of the elected officials in Westchester are solidly in favor of abortion rights. It's a textbook case of women with power turning the establishment upside down. A birder, Polly has traveled widely to observe birds in their habitat. She's no more afraid of snakes or spiders than she is of anti-abortion Senate Republicans.

Suzanne Seas (pseudonym) is an environmental policy analyst in Alaska. She is active in local social and environmental issues, and enjoys piano and outdoor recreation. This is her first published poem.

Sue Schlangen has a Master of Arts in Human Development with a strong emphasis in women's sexuality. She is a writer and educator on topics related to sexuality, such as body awareness and self-pleasuring.

Chandra Silva is an aspiring academic of sorts who spends her serious time in doctoral studies at Washington State University, Pullman, and her fun time in companionship with her life partner and the family's dogs, cats, and two ferrets, Puck and Harry. An ecofeminist, spiritual seeker, and champion of social justice, Chandra lectures by invitation on women's history, feminist theory, reproductive freedoms, and the matrix of systemic oppressions. She also edits a popular women's newsletter *Women With Wings* and teaches university classes on race, class, gender, family, and national identities.

Ashley Sovereign is a doctoral candidate in Counseling Psychology in Minneapolis. She has a long history of political activism in women's health issues, and has worked as a rape crisis counselor, sex educator, and abortion counselor. Ashley currently writes for sexingthepolitical.com, an online journal of third wave feminists on sexuality issues.

Chris Stark is a feminist writer, activist, speaker, artist, and poet. She has spoken to groups nationally and internationally, and her writing and artwork have been published in numerous anthologies and periodicals. In 1999 she co-founded Escape, an educational organization against prostitution and pornography. Currently, she teaches art and writing to battered and prostituted women while working toward an MFA in Writing.

DeDe Van Slyke received her Master of Arts degree in Counseling and Psychological Services from Saint Mary's University of Minnesota. She furthered her devotion to women's issues—particularly those of abuse and trauma—as a former volunteer domestic abuse advocate in the Hennepin County Attorney's Office. Now, in broader perspective, she contributes her expertise as Clinical Specialist with a Twin Cities mental health crises-center. While continuing to do special photography assignments, such as with *Our Choices, Our Lives: Unapologetic Writings on Abortion*, DeDe is now working toward her doctorate in Clinical Psychology.

Carla Vogel is a writer, storyteller, and community artist living in Minneapolis. She receives inspiration for her life and art from her five years as an abortion counselor.

INTRODUCTION

Krista Jacob, Editor

My abortions didn't make me more radical. People's feelings against them made me more radical. I didn't talk about my abortions when I was a kid, but after I became a grown woman, I did.[3]
Whoopi Goldberg, *The Choices We Made: Twenty-five women and men speak out about abortion*

If every woman who ever had an abortion, or even one-third of them, was willing to speak out about their experience—not in shame, but with honesty about where she was then, what she learned, and where she is now—this whole issue would heal a great deal faster.[4]
Dr. Christiane Northrup, *Women's Bodies, Women's Wisdom*

History shows us that the demand for abortion is not a modern issue. It has been well documented across cultures throughout recorded history that women have taken certain herbs, in tea infusions and otherwise, to expel unwanted tissue from their uteruses. In the absence of safe medical care, women have also brought injury to their bodies in attempts to cause miscarriages. Before 1973, the year abortion became legal in the United States, millions of American women sought help from "back alley" abortionists. Although sometimes successful, this approach frequently resulted in sterilization, permanent health problems, and even death. Such desperate measures to end an unwanted pregnancy combined with a belief that women must have complete and uncompromised control over their reproduction drove the women's liberation movement in its fight for safe, legal abortion. The US feminist movement of the 1960s and 1970s, often referred to as the "second wave" of feminism, helped make abortion legal in the United States.

Since its legalization, abortion has been one of our country's most contentious and controversial issues. It has been extensively argued from legal, political, and religious perspectives. But consistently, the debate about abortion hinges on a polarity between the pro-choice side, which supports reproductive choice for women (from adoption to parenthood to abortion) and advocates for legalized abortion and, the anti-choice or "pro-life" side, which deems abortion murder and has sought to impede women's access to abortion. Though this debate has highlighted important aspects of the issue, it posits abortion as only two-sided rather than multifaceted. In reality, abortion is a multi-layered choice that women from different countries, classes, and races, make everyday. By limiting our focus to the controversy *surrounding* abortion, we neglect, as individuals and as a greater community, to see the diversity of women's abortion experiences. For this reason, *Our Choices, Our Lives: Unapologetic Writings on Abortion* begins with a chapter of women's abortion testimonies.

My own choice to have an abortion was made during a difficult time in my life. I had recently moved to a new state in hopes of fulfilling my four-year goal of attending graduate school. Despite my optimism about these new possibilities, my move took a toll on my relationship with my then boyfriend. It quickly became apparent to both of us that our relationship couldn't survive the geographical separation. We spent our evenings bickering and second-guessing our commitment to one another. Completely disillusioned with our relationship, we decided to break up. The loss of this relationship was devastating for me: our lives were no longer intertwined, and the intimacy we had shared, or at least what I had thought was intimacy, quickly disappeared. Two weeks later, I found out I was pregnant. Since my boyfriend was no longer a source of support for me, emotional or otherwise, I found myself in the unfamiliar position of being alone and feeling isolated in my new environment. Though I had the good fortune to meet supportive people in my graduate school cohort, my relationships with them were new and lacked the depth I needed at such a critical time. Regardless, I didn't want to go to the clinic alone, so two newfound friends, Jennifer and Julie, agreed to go with me. They made me breakfast, drove me to the clinic, and waited with me in the lobby. While in the clinic, they held my hand and gave me support as I completed each step of the extensive abortion process, which included lab work, a counseling session, a physical exam, an ultra sound of my seven-week pregnancy, and, of course, the medical procedure itself.

My most powerful memory of that day is of two young women, possibly in their late teens, seated next to me in the waiting room. Sitting alone, each looked confused, frightened, and overwhelmed. One woman was compulsively reading and re-reading the information given to us by the clinic, while the other woman kept anxiously checking her pager as if waiting to hear from someone, possibly a friend or a boyfriend. As I watched these women, I felt sympathy for them—they seemed vulnerable, afraid, and completely alone without any visible support whatsoever. But as I thought about my own circumstances, despite the certainty of my choice and the support I felt from my new friends, I felt a strong connection with these two strangers. Educated, white, and in my mid twenties, I felt as alone, anxious, and overwhelmed as these women seemed to be. Looking back, I realize that as I watched them, fearful and alone, I was watching myself.

Upon my return from the clinic, my roommate Charles and I spent an ordinary afternoon together. We watched movies, ate ice cream, and, much to my relief, talked about everything *except* my abortion. I was physically and emotionally exhausted, grateful for a reprieve from the day's events. The following day, a woman from my neighborhood brought me dinner. Though we were not yet friends, I wanted to spend time with her. She was kind and seemed to want to spend time with me too, so I made tea and invited her to stay the afternoon. Seated at my kitchen table, she generously shared the stories of her three abortions. I listened attentively as she talked about the pregnancy that resulted from being raped as an adolescent. The humiliation and isolation from the rape combined with the judgment and scrutiny of her parents was palpable as she shared her painful experience. Her next two pregnancies had happened because three separate methods of birth control, including a vasectomy, had failed her and her husband. Together, they had chose to end their pregnancies because they were not financially or emotionally prepared to have a child. As she shared her stories with me, the unconditional and loving support of her husband stood in marked contrast to the cruel and judgmental behavior of her parents. At that moment, I saw clearly that the support a woman has, or the lack thereof, shapes the emotional and physical outcome of her abortion.

In retrospect, I believe that talking with her that afternoon was the thing that was most helpful to me in those first few weeks following my abortion. I'm certain that my commitment to hearing and sharing women's stories is a result of my experience that afternoon. For it is through our connections with one another that we grow and heal from the challenging life experiences that many women share. These relationships, when recognized and valued, can be a critical source of our empowerment.

I was not conflicted about whether or not to have an abortion; it was a decision I was sure about. Rather, my grief was caused by the circumstances that surrounded my abortion: the end of my relationship, my financial instability, moving away from my friends and the place that had been my home for four years, and feeling alone in a new place and graduate program. Since my spiritual beliefs embrace abortion as a moral choice, I was not confused about the morality of my choice. For me, having an abortion was an act of grace as well as the best way for me to honor myself. I do not believe I "murdered a baby" as the anti-choice protesters would accuse; rather, my choice to end my pregnancy opened up new possibilities for me as a young woman and allowed me to have a fuller and richer life, free from the burdens of unwanted motherhood. My abortion allowed me to close the doors on the life I did not want and to pursue the personal and professional goals that were important to me. Unlike generations of women before me, I had a legal, medically safe, and dignified abortion. I wasn't forced to leave the country or surrender my physical safety to a complete stranger, which allowed me to fully embrace, without fear of physical harm, my abortion experience.[5]

Women's emotional responses to abortion are as varied as the issue itself. Ending an unwanted pregnancy is not always a painful choice or experience; on the contrary, many women derive empowerment from their choice and view it as a means of personal growth that deepens their self-awareness. The abortion experience illuminates new truths for some women and provides clarity and insights they previously did not have. For example, I've witnessed women leave abusive relationships and make other productive, life-changing decisions as a result of their abortion experience.

On the other hand, for many reasons, there are women who experience varying degrees of trauma or extreme grief subsequent to their abortion. They might feel guilty for having had an abortion because they perceive abortion as ending a life, or, more commonly, as ending the *possibility* of a life. What's more, since our society dictates that women feel guilty each time they consider their own needs before the needs of others, some women feel guilty for *not* feeling guilty or remorseful. Further, many women are shamed by the stigma assigned to women who have sex (slut, whore, immoral, etc.). In addition to feeling shame about ending their pregnancies, these women feel guilt for having had sex in the first place. They might blame themselves for getting "caught up in the moment" and not using birth control; in fact, in some instances, women even blame themselves when birth control methods fail them.

Based on my experience as an abortion counselor and as a sexuality educator, I've found that most women experience a contradictory mixture of feelings: the pain of grief and loss coupled with the promise of relief and hope.

For most women, an unplanned pregnancy raises every life issue imaginable, causing a kind of existential crisis for them and possibly their partners. Upon finding out that they are pregnant, they might (re)examine their support systems, religious views, financial resources, intimate relationships, future aspirations (personal and professional), circumstances surrounding the pregnancy (such as sexual assault or failed birth control), and so on. Despite the admonitions of conservative-minded people who accuse women of making thoughtless and capricious decisions to end pregnancies, the litany of factors women consider before they choose abortion is extensive. Anyone who dismisses women as selfish or irresponsible is seriously out of touch with the processes women go through when choosing abortion.

On a political level, many women who choose abortion are not fully aware of the historical fight for legalized abortion, nor are they aware of present-day political activism to protect a woman's right to choose. Like me, however, many women are (further) politicized by their abortion experience. Whether it was the enforcement of insulting waiting periods, inadequate medical insurance coverage, or groups of zealous protestors who harassed them as they entered the clinic, many women's abortion experiences served as a catalyst for new political awareness. Nonetheless, the legal status of abortion has mistakenly led many people to believe that the right to choose abortion is safe and guarded; the harsh reality is that abortion is less accessible today than it was in 1975. The members of the conservative movement against abortion rights are in full swing; and by tactics such as abortion restrictions and clinic terrorism, they have eroded abortion rights and gained considerable ground for their misogynist movement. Our activism is more necessary than ever.

My sincere hope is that providing a forum for women to share their abortion experiences as well as perspectives from those who work on the frontlines of activism and the clinics, will help enrich the myriad ways our culture views this multifaceted issue. When my colleague and friend Ashley Sovereign and I first envisioned this book, we wanted it to help fill some of the gaps that exist between personal experience and political activism, because we strongly believe that abortion rights activism must always be informed by women's abortion experiences.

And, lastly, I hope this book will illuminate the many faces of abortion and challenge those who harshly judge women as immoral, irresponsible, promiscuous, or selfish. As *Our Choices, Our Lives: Unapologetic Writings on Abortion* reveals, women are indeed intelligent, moral, and compassionate creatures, fully capable of deciding when or if they want to have a child.

In this spirit, I have chosen to introduce these brave and beautifully written political and personal essays with the affirming prose of Anne Baker and Jean Stewart Berg. *Women Know* validates the morality and intellect of women and the deep personal belief they have in themselves and the children they may or may not choose to have.

PART I

ABORTION TESTIMONIES: BEFORE AND AFTER LEGAL ABORTION

WOMEN KNOW

Anne Baker and Jean Stewart Berg

We women know when it is or is not the right time to bring a child into the world.

We use our heads and our hearts to see clearly the pros and cons of our three choices: parenting, placing for adoption, or having an abortion.

We know better than anyone else what we can and cannot handle emotionally, physically, financially, and mentally.

We have wisdom enough to know our own limits and strength enough to admit them.

We know when the choice of abortion can prevent the harsh consequences of bringing a child into the world when we are not ready or able to do our child justice.

We act out of compassion when we wait to have a child until the time when we can give it the kind of life every child deserves.

We act out of love when we consider what we would be taking away from the child or children we already have if we brought another child into our family now.

We take care of our mental health by making decisions that limit the strain we place upon ourselves and those we love.

We take care of our physical health by considering our medical history and the risks that come with pregnancy, labor, and delivery.

We take care of our spiritual well being each in our own way, trusting our faith to provide:
Infinite Love
Complete Understanding
Unlimited Forgiveness
Boundless Compassion

We think clearly when we call our abortion decision one of "self-care" rather than calling ourselves "selfish." We must care for ourselves before we can take care of another human being.

We see clearly, beyond a well-wisher's words, "I'll help you out if you have the baby…" We know that the responsibility for raising the child will fall squarely on our own shoulders.

We have foresight enough to know that "having a baby" doesn't stop with infancy. It means raising a child who will need our financial support, time, and attention for as long as it takes the child to become an independent adult.

Women throughout all time and throughout the world have made the decision to have an abortion, whether or not abortion was safe and legal. Women have risked their own lives to avoid bearing a child they could not adequately care for.

Women in the past drank teas made from parts of plants known to cause abortion. In desperation, some inserted long, thin objects into their cervixes and others douched with poisonous liquids to cause an abortion. Some methods cost women their lives.

Childbirth, miscarriage, and abortion are all part of women's lives. Women of childbearing age from every generation, occupation, income level, race, and religion have had abortions including great-grandmothers, grandmothers, mothers, great-aunts, aunts, sisters, daughters, best friends, teachers, ministers, doctors, and daycare workers.

And when others use television commercials, billboards, bumper stickers, speeches, and sermons to make us feel guilty about having an abortion,

> **We women know the truth:**
> **That given certain circumstances**
> **Abortion is the most morally responsible**
> **And loving choice we can make.**

Reprinted with the permission of The Hope Clinic for Women, Ltd.
© 1997 The Hope Clinic for Women, Ltd.

BEFORE ROE V. WADE

CHILDHOOD PAUSE

Carol Harder

This is my story. I am telling it because there are young women who don't know what it was like before abortion was legalized. They are unaware of the suffering and they take their right to choose for granted.

I became pregnant in 1969, at the age of fifteen. When my period didn't come, I contacted a local doctor chosen from the phone book. After swearing him to secrecy, he agreed to be my referring physician for a pregnancy test. For the younger generation's information, we did not have at-home pregnancy tests. Since they could only use a first morning urine sample, the next day, before school, I collected a urine sample in a sterilized baby food jar and carried it in my purse throughout the entire school day. I convinced a friend's older brother to drive me to the hospital so I could take the urine sample to the lab. Then, I walked home. The next evening, I phoned the doctor at his home for the results. He said, "You'd better have a talk with your parents."

One option we had in those days was to be sent away to a maternity home for the duration of the pregnancy (I knew a girl who had done this at age twelve) and give the child up for adoption. I attempted to contact the Salvation Army's Home for Unwed Mothers, but didn't have the nerve to complete the call. In those times (if the father was present and accepting responsibility), a marriage license was generally issued along with a death certificate for the sacrificial rabbit. I lived in the typical "Ozzie & Harriet" household of the sixties, so the immediate solution was to marry the father, who agreed, though he desired neither a wife nor a child. He was nineteen and abusive toward me. A few weeks after we married, my parents came to realize that the situation was intolerable, and they brought me home. Soon thereafter, I filed for divorce.

My parents broached the subject of abortion. At first I was horrified. I always thought it was wrong (after all, it was illegal) but eventually I decided I didn't have any other option. I had a relative living in another state who had some connections with people involved with illegal activities, and she arranged for me to meet with an abortionist. The procedure was explained to us. It involved piercing through the cervix and forcing saline solution into the uterus to induce a miscarriage. It was described as extremely painful and having a high risk of uterine perforation. It would be performed at a local motel, and we were advised that if there were any complications at all, the anonymous abortionist would disappear, and we would be on our own. I returned home, still pregnant.

A local politician (who was a friend of my father's) referred me to a physician. He was an unscrupulous character, known around town for writing excessive prescriptions for pain relievers and tranquilizers. I assumed he would perform a safe abortion on me. But, instead he sexually abused me during pelvic exams, and insisted that I tell him I loved him (while he puffed on a big cigar) during these exams. I never told anyone, because I was afraid he would refuse to help me if I told. His methods included giving me hallucinogenic drugs, instructing me to jump off chairs and ladders, and sending me on long bumpy car rides. When none of this worked, he gave us a phone number to call for a more direct method.

Within a week, my father and I were downtown late at night with two hundred dollars in unmarked twenty-dollar bills, and an address in hand. We found the house we were looking for, and went inside. There was an elderly Black woman there, a very motherly type, who tried to soothe me. I marveled at the pictures of her grown children, some in military uniforms, on tables in her living room. I was terrified, and hadn't been told what to expect. The woman counted the money and guided me to a dark bedroom in the back of the house, where she had me lie on the bed. There was a young man standing in the corner by a window, acting as a lookout. I could only make out his silhouette. Next, she told me to lie still and quiet, and she produced a long catheter. She pushed it through my cervix, and continued to force a foot or so of the catheter into my uterus. It wasn't terribly painful, but I couldn't stop shaking. Within fifteen minutes, I was on my way home, but still pregnant.

The doctor was called, and he gave instructions to my father. I was to keep the catheter in place, and it would cause irritation or infection, which would eventually make me abort. Within a few days, the catheter was expelled, and I managed to put it back in myself. By this time, I was more than three months along. Soon I began having contractions. They continued for about twelve hours, and I started passing very large blood clots. I felt an extreme fullness, grabbed a handful of tissues and there it was. I was shocked to see a fully formed fetus. I called out for my parents to help me. I was put to bed, and my father buried the fetus in the backyard. The sense of relief was overwhelming, but so was the sadness.

Infection was inevitable, and the next day I was hemorrhaging. The clots were so large that I labored with each one. I became extremely weak from the blood loss, but we were all afraid to seek medical attention for fear of being arrested. The doctor refused our calls once he knew I was in medical trouble. My parents were afraid that I was going to die so they took me to the emergency room. The nurse kept asking me how long it had been since I had had the abortion. I just kept answering that I hadn't had an abortion. She finally said they couldn't help me if I didn't tell the truth. But I couldn't tell and risk sending my parents to jail.

I don't know what happened in the emergency room after that. I only remember waking up after having had a D&C (Dilation and Curettage). It was a horrible experience that I would never wish for anyone. My family and I did not suffer legal repercussions, but, sadly, the elderly Black woman had performed the same procedure on another young girl who wasn't as fortunate as I had been. A few months later, she was sentenced to prison for ten years, and the disgusting doctor was spending his weekends in prison.

I am forty-four years old now, and a few years ago my youngest daughter became pregnant. She had her pregnancy terminated in a supportive female-staffed clinic. Our personal gynecologist was affiliated with the clinic. We had had no idea, as she had to keep it secret in order to protect her private practice from retaliation in our backward small town. My daughter was fine and back to her normal routine the next day. The difficult part for her was making the decision to terminate the pregnancy. How wonderful that once her decision was made, she had access to safe, supportive medical care.

Ironically, she had not been interested in attending a pro-choice rally with me several years before because she had felt that we would never be in danger of losing our right to choose. She knew nothing of the deaths and suffering of women in the time before Roe v. Wade. I am afraid that too many young women don't believe that their right to have a legal and safe abortion can be taken away from them. In their lifetime, they have always had the right to choose, and they can't imagine what it would be like without it.

There will always be abortions, legal or illegal. We deserve the right to reproductive freedom. The anti-abortion groups (I won't call them pro-life, because they've never shown any concern for the quality of the lives of children) base their views on religious beliefs. The fact that others may not share their beliefs is irrelevant to them. The pro-choice rally I attended in the eighties (joined by my eldest daughter and my mother) was protested against by members of local churches, who surrounded us in the town-square with their signs and songs. It was a peaceful protest, and we even conversed with some members from our own church who were in attendance. They said they would pray for us. I wish all anti-abortion protesters could limit their protests to such peaceful methods.

In the late seventies, I worked in an office complex with an adjoining building where an abortion clinic had opened. I was happy to see them open, and helped coordinate their lease agreement with the building's landlord. The protests began even before the clinic opened. Leaving the building complex required driving through a group of protesters holding signs with pictures of bloody late term fetuses, and chanting religious slogans. They harassed every woman who entered the building complex. The clinic was in operation for a few years, then someone set fire to it. They rebuilt, and were burned to the ground. They relocated their facilities to a more progressive city, located about thirty miles away.

 I know that my personal experience may pale against the tragedies experienced by other women. I was lucky, I had a supportive family, and after I had my abortion, I was able to go on with my life. Many women did not have this luxury. But, now we are in danger of having our rights stripped from us. We have religious freedom in this country, but we are subject to the demands of religious zealots who wish to control our reproductive freedom. Women must know how it was before we had this freedom, so they will value and actively protect it.

MOTHERLODE, MOTHERLORE

Kathleen George Kearney

Discovered photograph, circa 1900

you hid the abortion well,
just like the old woman with the cracked jar of lye
and the hot sterile instrument
told you
you should.
You didn't scream, like your oldest cousin told you
she did
when her married boyfriend drove her over the state line
to the doctor who had his little boy holding the lantern
and running the bucket out back to dump out by the hog's trough.
You didn't tell your mother
and you didn't go into a pale shock,
and you didn't bleed to death
right then and there,
leaving the old woman with an empty shot glass
and an amazed expression
on her tired face.

You tucked away the momentary agony which released you,
the liberating gulp of whiskey she insisted
you have,
the instrument of salvation
you pray each day in your mind
never to see
(it was just a knitting needle held over a hot stove).

And you didn't run to the police
and you didn't go to the county hospital
and tell a story about how
you fell down the stairs
and you didn't know you were carrying
and please don't tell your husband,
because he'd be devastated.

You certainly didn't tell your pastor at the Sunday picnic,
or the pastor's wife,
when she asked you why your weren't eating,
you didn't let the timbermen
find you floating like a sad leaf in the creek
north of the saw mill,
like they did the Lawrence girl
when she was just fifteen.
And you didn't try to stop the bleeding
with the concoctions the Dakota midwife
once told your sister would do the trick:
with pennyroyal and oak leaves,
some green wood from a willow,
a little stolen quinine.

You hid the abortion well.
You took your place beside the husband,
on evening walks,
at mumming pianos,
slipped in the bed and created a diversion.
Hid the new slope of your belly,
the clots you didn't pass.
You hid the septic womb,
where your dreaming hope
cried and listed like a boat on a storm.

And when you died,
the doctor and the husband hid the cause,
the doctor telling the mortician it was a
bad miscarriage,
the husband telling the children you
went to god
because you loved them just   so   much.

After the funeral,
your first girl hid the picture
taken at the end of summer,
when there was nothing yet to hide.
The girl stows it underneath her pillow,
to weep into at night,
a witness to the days before the abortion,
when the baby son wore his pants short,
and the second daughter turned her face away,
proud and gorgeous.

The first daughter
(the one you named after your beloved great-aunt)
is the one who smiles freely,
never imagining
it can end this way:
a mother will explode into scarlet
and be lost forever,
destiny hangs on the edge of a shot of whiskey
and freedom is bittersweet,
the autumn comes with a crisp slice of darkness,
and abortions get hidden.

UNEXPECTED BLESSING

Reverend Mary Beth O'Halloran

Only once or twice in most lifetimes do we experience life-changing events. Undoubtedly, abortion changed the direction of my life. The unplanned (and unwanted) pregnancy itself would have changed my life, regardless of my decision. Marriage to an alcoholic drifter, single parenthood, or abortion—all my options were earth shaking. But I chose abortion.

It was before Roe v. Wade. I was twenty-nine, single, and had a graduate level education. I had just lost my job as a laborer in a cardboard box factory. I was living in my hometown, in a rented house, with the father of my pregnancy, whenever he drifted into town.

Before I became pregnant, the landlord revoked my lease because he wanted to give the house to his son as a wedding present. Just as I moved back into my rigidly Catholic parents' house, I found out I was pregnant. I had morning sickness twenty hours a day, but I discovered that consuming a steady flow of Oreo cookies kept the nausea under control. I was careful to hide the eating from my father because he was a doctor and might become suspicious. I also could not risk going to any local doctors, even under an assumed name, for fear my father would find out. Ironically, I was taking a night course on health care delivery for low-income families, so I learned about a medical clinic two hours away that offered a sliding-scale fee.

I was already certain I was pregnant. I was a stomach sleeper, and I could feel the fetus, however tiny it must have been, inside of me. When the doctor confirmed the pregnancy, I asked for information on abortion. First a nurse, then a doctor kindly attempted to make sure that abortion was really what I wanted. There was no doubt in my mind or in my heart. My choice was certain from the moment I suspected I was pregnant.

I had attended Catholic schools my entire life. In fact, after high school I entered a convent. Though I left, I fully intended to return someday. When I found out I was pregnant, my Catholic education boomeranged. I thought about all the moral arguments against abortion, from both my theology and philosophy classes. Abortion was murder; it was a grievous sin. Even a priest couldn't hear my confession; only a bishop or someone with a higher ranking could absolve me for my sin of abortion. The church's stand—*my* church's stand—was absolutely clear. So was my decision to have the abortion.

The abortion itself was difficult. I was alone; the father of my pregnancy said he didn't approve. I used the last of my earnings from my laborer job and drove an hour north, to my father's hometown, to a clinic. I was afraid, the procedure was painful, and the medical people were impatient with my fear. I stayed the night alone and afraid of bleeding to death in a cheap motel without a phone. The next day I started driving from town to town looking for work—this was the excuse I had given my parents for being away overnight. The whole experience was unpleasant, but I was truly lucky. My pregnancy occurred before Roe v. Wade, but I had a safe and sanitary abortion.

Whichever option I chose would have changed my life forever. I could have been married to a loser, raising a child in poverty. I could have been a single mom, raising a child in poverty, working meaningless, futureless jobs to support us. My father, who was always holier than the church, would never have forgiven me for having had sex in the first place, so I wouldn't have had any support from my family.

As I've said, choosing abortion altered my life, even though it was the least life-changing of the decisions. For several years after leaving the convent, I had stayed in the Catholic Church. I loved the Church; I still intended to return to the convent. But I found its social teachings offensive, specifically its stance on the Vietnam war, birth control, individual conscience, and women's roles. But the final straw, so to speak, was the realization that the church considered my conscientious decision to have an abortion to be an unforgivable sin.

My choice was made in the best conscience. Factors included my inability to earn a living for myself much less to provide a child with a stable and secure environment, doubts about the genetic inheritance from my unstable and alcoholic boyfriend, and a choice for quality over quantity of life. My reasons, my conscience, had no relevance to the church. It deemed me an outcast and found my actions to be unforgivable. I knew I could no longer be Catholic. I left the church totally on the day I had the abortion.

Today I am an ordained minister, fulfilling my religious vocation in a liberal Protestant denomination. My current church recognizes the right of women to follow their own consciences and to make their own choices about their bodies. As a volunteer religious counselor for women who are trying to decide about abortion, I hear repeatedly the fear that the church has used to control women—fear of hell, fear of public excommunication, fear of doing what our bodies and our consciences tell us is right.

Abortion changed my life in ways I didn't anticipate. It drove me from a church that did not accept me as a moral woman with a sincere and developed conscience. It opened the door to a life of religious service that honors who I am, and allows me to serve as a religious woman who has had an abortion.

PATTY

Polly Rothstein
Former President, Westchester Coalition for Legal Abortion, Inc.

I am from Connecticut, where birth control was illegal while I was growing up. Women lobbied for decades to change these restrictive laws, but lawmakers refused. So what did women do? The lucky ones' husbands or partners used condoms. The unlucky ones had babies, shotgun marriages, went to homes for unwed mothers, or got illegal abortions. One poor soul graduated from high school with me in 1954, her belly-of-shame too big to hide. She was scorned for her pregnancy and heavy makeup. I still feel for her.

In 1958, age twenty-one, fresh out of college and very naïve, I moved to Cambridge, Massachusetts to share an apartment with my friend Patty and to get a job. As I was about to move in, Patty shattered the peace by announcing she was pregnant. At the time, both birth control and abortion were illegal in Massachusetts.

We couldn't say the bad word "abortion." Instead we said, "get rid of it," and knew we had to find a way to do so. We started calling everyone that Patty knew "for a name," anyone who could help her to obtain an abortion. Any name would do; we didn't ask about qualifications or safety, much less ask for a doctor. We were frantic to end it. A male acquaintance gave us the name of Dr. Robert Spencer in Ashland, Pennsylvania, and instructed Patty to tell him she needed treatment for "vaginal discharge." We failed at the time to see the humor in going from Cambridge to coal country for treatment of vaginal discharge. Dr. Spencer informed us that the procedure would take two visits, he then told us which motel to call, and where to park our car.

Dr. Spencer's office was weird, or at the very least unusual. The walls and ceilings were covered with plaques, mostly wooden ones containing slogans or poems, usually sold as souvenirs to tourists at resorts or big parks. The one I remember most vividly was of a vase, which, as you stared at the negative spaces became the silhouette of two faces. We avoided eye contact with the other people in the waiting room, all of us scared and unwilling to swap how-I-got-here stories, seek or give solace, or make small talk. Instead, Patty and I whispered to each other.

In those years there were no instant pregnancy tests. One waited until she missed her second period, then it took weeks for diagnosis. The method of abortion was Dilation and Curettage (D&C) performed many weeks into pregnancy, mostly without anesthesia.

Dr. Spencer was white-haired and kindly. If he tried to reassure us, he failed. He packed Patty's vagina with something to dilate her cervix and told us to come back to his office in the morning. I remember the town was a typical small town, but I don't recall having dinner or staying at the motel. The next morning at Dr. Spencer's office, I feared the worst when he took her away and put me in a small recovery room to wait. The room had a chair, cot, and black-covered book: *Crimes of Passion*. Anxiously, I repeatedly rehearsed my explanation to Patty's stern and formal parents about where we had gone and why Patty had died.

Eventually, Dr. Spencer brought Patty in, draped over his shoulder in a fireman's carry. He had given her general anesthesia. He gently lowered her onto the cot, and when I saw that her eyes were rolled back so the whites showed, I knew, at least, that she was still alive. Later she regained consciousness and rested while Dr. Spencer checked her and gave her post-op instructions and antibiotics. The charge for everything was fifty dollars.

Later I learned that Dr. Spencer was the town doctor beloved by all, protected by the police, and a hero to women from around the nation. He's the subject of several book chapters about illegal abortions, and he was featured in a recent documentary. Women still put flowers on his grave. I have heard that he had a file of letters from desperate women seeking abortions, and passionate letters of thanks from women whom he helped. He's often referred to as "the angel of Ashland."

I didn't know how good we had it at Dr. Spencer's until I heard others' tales of the difficulties and time lost getting together huge sums of cash that others were forced to pay. I've heard countless horror stories of the back-alley butchers; being driven around blindfolded so as not to know where the abortion took place; rape or sodomy by the creepy, smelly abortionist before he performed the abortion; the tied hands; the mouth stuffed to muffle the cries; the threats to "Shut up or you're out of here"; the unclean table and instruments; the horrible pain; the hemorrhaging; the lies told to the hospital emergency room; and so on.

I left Cambridge in 1959 to get married. Though illegal, birth control was available in NYC. I went to the Margaret Sanger clinic for a stressful and undignified session. I had to bring a doctor's note affirming that I was indeed getting married. I felt like the criminal I was, and the liar I was not. But a friend's story tops mine: after being fit for a diaphragm, she watched the female doctor poke a hole in it so she could use it only for insertion practice, and would have to return for a new one the day before her wedding.

I found out about the strategy of some Connecticut women when, as a mother of toddlers in 1965, I became a Planned Parenthood volunteer. I learned that the clinic was founded to serve Connecticut women, many of whom caught the New Haven line train to Port Chester, walked a block to the clinic for an exam and "supplies," and boarded the train to return home clutching a plain brown bag with the bootleg diaphragm or pills. (The first oral contraceptives were dispensed that year.)

Also in 1965, the Supreme Court threw out Connecticut's ban on contraceptives, interpreting the Constitution to give *married* couples the right to privacy in such matters. (Yes, 1965) In 1972, the Court let single women in on it, and the next year, on January 22, 1973, the Court ruled that abortion was included in the privacy right.

Patty's abortion pointed me to the Planned Parenthood clinic. Fear of the loss of abortion rights and birth control led me inexorably to abortion politics around 1970. My hope for the future is that women who come of age now, when Roe seems long ago, learn what so many women from their mothers' and grandmothers' generation went through when both birth control and abortion were illegal. And, most importantly, that they work politically to protect these precious rights.

INTERVIEW WITH FRAN

Michelle Menter

In my last year of college, I conducted a series of interviews with women who had chosen abortion. I did it to find myself. I'd had an abortion and it left me numb. I couldn't feel anything about my choice. I really trusted that I'd made the right decision but I could hear the pro-life voices in my head. I responded by shutting down; I moved forward without feeling.

On the day of my abortion while sitting in the clinic's waiting room, it occurred to me how alone we all were. We were all there, at the clinic, doing the same thing, in the same place, but we were miles apart. And I thought that just a smile would be enough to bring comfort, but no one smiled, and it probably wouldn't have been enough anyway. So I decided to conduct a series of interviews with women about their abortion experience. The following is one of those interviews.

While conducting these interviews, I sometimes saw my own story reflected, sometimes not. But, today, I am reclaiming my experience for myself. I am beginning to feel again…[6]

Interview

Fran found me in front of the library, where I was nervously rechecking my interview questions. Over the phone I had described myself as "a redhead with a bike" and she said she'd be "the only white-haired, old lady around." She had a warm smile and reassuring disposition; she was comfortable telling her story and it felt good to hear her tell it.

My interview with Fran set itself apart from the rest of the interviews not so much because she had her abortion before Roe v. Wade, but because, unlike the other (post-Roe v. Wade) women, she wasn't struggling with guilt and self-doubt. She'd had more than thirty years to reflect on her decision so maybe that's why she seemed so comfortable with her decision, but I don't think that's the only reason.

Fran could afford a "respectable abortion," nothing like the coat hanger/kitchen table stuff I've heard about from others. In fact her procedure sounded a lot like the rest of ours, notwithstanding the flight to Puerto Rico. I think the big difference is that her decision was supported by her husband and by the social environment in which she made her choice. She was very sure she wanted an abortion, the fact that it was illegal had very little influence on her decision. Here's her interview: Thank you, Fran, for sharing your story.

Fran:

I am sixty-nine-years old. I had the abortion in 1965 or 66—that's pre Roe vs. Wade. I was already married; I had three children, my youngest child at that point was five or six. My husband had been having some problems at his job when we unexpectedly found ourselves pregnant. Both of us were very concerned.

I thought, 'Oh my God, I'm going to be sixty-years-old and I'm still going to have children around me who need money for college and other things.' My husband was shook up about the job and supporting the family he already had. We felt that since we already had three wonderful children, we didn't want any more. We had two boys and a girl; it was perfect. Why would we want more children?

First, I called a friend who had a lot of contacts in Manhattan and was in social work. I thought that she might know somebody, a doctor maybe, who did abortions. She called me back and said that her contacts were no longer available.

I went to my regular internist with whom I had been a patient for twenty some years. He indirectly suggested that he'd had experiences with an abortionist in Puerto Rico. He suggested that we contact him.

I then went to see a psychiatrist with whom I'd had a relationship. I told him the story, and he said that he'd be willing to go before the hospital committee to advocate for me to have an abortion. He didn't think it was a good idea, however, because it would probably take months. Though I was very early in my pregnancy, (I was one of those people who knew immediately if I was pregnant), I wanted the abortion sooner than later. The psychiatrist then said, 'If I were you, I'd go to Puerto Rico,' which we eventually did.

My husband made the arrangements, and we flew to Puerto Rico. I was terrified during the flight. I'm not a particularly religious person, I don't believe in a God who cares about me as an individual, but I had this anxious feeling of 'Oh boy.'

Once we were in Puerto Rico, we checked into a hotel and the next day we went to the abortion clinic. Looking at the waiting room walls, I saw that the doctor apparently had gotten his medical degree in Mexico. The room was filled with people, mostly Americans. This was clearly one of the most traumatic events in my life, which is why I remember it so clearly. Next, we went into his office, and immediately the price increased from what he had previously quoted to my husband. But we were in no position to quibble at that point, and the doctor knew it.

It's fascinating to reflect on this experience. I remember sitting in the room and looking at the women who were there—some alone, some with friends, some with parents, everybody looking terrified. Fortunately, this experience was brief.

Next he gave me some kind of local anesthetic in the genital area. I was awake throughout the whole procedure. Next I remember feeling a lot of pain, and he started to scrape out my uterus. I remember you could hear the scraping and feel the scraping, but this part wasn't painful. Then, it was over. The doctor ushered me into a room with cots, where there were five or six other women. I was supposed to stay there until I felt I could get up and walk out.

I've always felt that I had an abortion under the best of all possible circumstances. My husband was with me and was supportive; we had the money to do it: to fly there and to pay the fee, even after it was increased.

We stayed at the Condato Beach. My husband had a friend in Puerto Rico who was a doctor, and told us to watch for infection, and to call immediately if I had a temperature. He said he'd use his influence to get us into the medical center, if needed.

Yet, despite all of this, when I think of what we women, especially those with less than I had, had to go through, I see what an awful situation it was. It has made me a continuing supporter of a woman's right to choose.

The people who were my friends and colleagues at the time always thought they could get an abortion if they needed one. The terrible part was not knowing what you were getting yourself into, because, since there was no regulation of the doctor or the clinic, you didn't know if he really had a medical degree or if he was safe. I remember when I had my abortion, I didn't see him sterilize the instruments or even wash his hands, and I don't know if he really had a medical degree from Mexico. And I had no control over any of it.

It was the unknown, the thought that I might be putting myself in harm's way, and that I might actually die from the abortion, that was so terrifying. The fear was awful, and having to deal with all of this when the important issue was that I knew I didn't want a child, or, for other women, that they didn't want a child at that particular time. I believe my situation, as a married woman, was more typical since, from my experience, it seemed like more married women were getting abortions than unmarried women. Yet, oddly, what mostly got talked about were the unmarried women.

I remember I thought it was ridiculous for other people to prevent somebody like myself, who was educated and thoughtful and already had three children, from having an abortion. I also thought it was ridiculous for them to judge me and think that I couldn't decide what was medically sound for me. My anger wasn't at other people in my life, rather it was at the fact that I couldn't go to the medical authorities to do what had to be done.

I want people to understand that individuals should have a right to examine their lives and decide what is best for them, especially since the individual is the one who best understands her own life and future. It's important for every woman to make her own choice without outside restrictions.

AFTER ROE V. WADE

SPEAKING MY TRUTH

Chandra Silva

My silences had not protected me. Your silence will not protect you. But for every real word spoken, for every attempt I had ever made to speak those truths for which I am still seeking, I had made contact with other women while we examined the words to fit a world in which we all believed, bridging our differences.[7]
Audre Lorde, *Sister Outsider: Essays and Speeches by Audre Lorde.*

There are just some things that you flat-out keep to yourself and never tell anybody. In all of my years, I have tucked away more than a few torrid tales. But, I always thought you were supposed to be able to tell your family doctor anything.

When I was growing up, our family doctor was a large Black man with a bald spot that resembled a skullcap. I remember having a sense of reverence about him because he was Black. I often thought about how challenging it must have been for him to get through the rigors of medical school, being Black and having to work twice as hard as his colleagues to be taken seriously as a medical student. I thought he had to be a good doctor, despite my feelings of discomfort since I always thought he looked at me in a predatory way. He seemed to make eye contact in a way that suggested he wasn't listening at all—instead he was thinking of what he was going to say next.

What I know now is that sometime in the summer of 1977, I got pregnant and he missed the diagnosis by several weeks. I have no memory of even thinking I could be pregnant when I found myself going back and forth between appointments to the doctor's office trying to discover why I wasn't menstruating. I wasn't having sex, and I told him that. After each visit, I'd begin a week's prescription of birth control pills to bring on my period. The subject of a possible pregnancy never came up—until the last visit.

With the snap of his glove, and a quick pelvic exam, my doctor confirmed that I was about six weeks pregnant. His next instructions were for me to submit a urine sample. He needed a "pee test, to be sure." His look was suspicious, and his deep, almost black eyes penetrated my shallow nervousness. He studied me with the staunch conviction of a father. I was motionless. By the time I rushed across the hall to the bathroom, with my "pee cup" in hand, I felt myself simultaneously inside and outside of my body. I remember I thought the worst. I couldn't breathe. My mind was on full alert and somewhere else, so when I sat down to fill up the cup, I missed it altogether. I had no pee for the cup. In a panic, I reached underneath the basin stand and grabbed some toilet bowl cleaner, giving a quick shot to my specimen cup. I added a little water to make it look more like urine. This was the sample I left at the desk. I was a desperate and scared child.

Not ten minutes later he returned to the room. "Yep, uh-huh, like I thought...the test is positive."

"But you bastard," I thought, "I faked the sample."

He was a dead, cold liar. But in an instant, he squashed any opportunity that I might have had to contest his results by moving his big, stern body to just inches from my face. Sternly, he told me, "I suggest you get your ass home, tell your parents, and get yourself an abortion. And do it right now. These are my instructions to you as your doctor: You listen to me here and now, girlie. If I was your father, I'd get you in for an abortion so fast it would make your head spin, and don't think for one second about any of your so-called options because if my daughter refused, I would kick her out of the house. So don't you go thinking differently."

I was frozen stiff. I thought I was dead. To a fifteen-year-old girl, this is the weight of the world. Maddeningly, images of sheer fear and terror ripped through my mind. Time began to stop and start in visions of telling my parents. That fear. They would blame me solely. But their eyes, those eyes. I knew exactly how they were going to take it. I'd seen it before, only this time I could imagine a visual burning at the stake. Yes, I knew it would be ten times worse than other offenses, like when I took the car, or didn't come home at night. The nostril-flaring, deep glaring, penetrating, soul-piercing, evil eyes were something I tried to avoid at all costs.

The first person I told was my boyfriend Jon. It was around Halloween or so, and we'd been dating since September. In that time, we'd had sex once. This was my choice and not Jon's, for if it had been up to him, we'd have been a lot more sexual. The truth was that I hated the guy. He was six years older than my fifteen-year-old self. But he wined me, dined me, turned me on to marijuana, and got me into bars for free. Somehow I got past his cigarette-smoking, acne-scarred unattractiveness and the experience of our first date (must've been the movie ticket and Schlitz Bulls). At the end of our first date, I found myself parked with Jon in his big white Ford truck atop a high point overlooking the city, and we began to make out. But he kept forcing my head down towards his crotch, and I hated the pressure. I hated being forced to do anything, and he kept putting his hands on my head. Down, down he wanted me to go, but I wouldn't. So I consented to sex. I allowed him to fuck me instead, right there in the front seat of his truck. I would have done anything so I didn't have to go down on him. I just didn't know I had options. I couldn't stand up for myself.

When I told Jon that I'd seen a doctor who confirmed my six-week pregnancy, he made a big jerk of himself. Whereas I suffered terribly on the inside, he let it all out. He stomped around the perimeter of his big white Ford truck, kicked the tires, screamed at me for being so irresponsible, and then sat down on the curb, crying. He said, "My dad will kill me."

There is no perfect time to tell your parents something this drastic. I figured it would be better if Jon and I told my mother first, and then she could break the news to my dad. I had rehearsed it in my mind over and over; yes, my mother would sneer and loudly insult me, and my dad would try to be pragmatic. He'd let my mom do the lecturing.

They reacted just as I suspected they would; but they added the final blow: I "have no choice in the matter." Abortion was our answer. It was "the only answer, so deal with it." As a matter of fact, my mom said she'd make the appointment for me and told me to sit back and wait for further instructions. Jon was told to go home, silently, to his upper-class family. Before he left, my parents consoled him and assured us they would not tell Jon's parents, "nor hold him to any responsibility besides possibly holding my hand through the procedure." What a noble deed for a tall knight. He was, after all, almost twenty-two and trying to launch a respectable business for himself, based on his father's interests.

On the day of my appointment, Jon and I decided that I should get "really stoned" before the procedure. "Yeah," he assured me, "Get blasted, babe." I had it in my mind, too, that marijuana would be a numbing, medicating crutch for comfort. Getting stoned that morning turned out to be the stupidest thing I could have done, because the information I received in those first few minutes of my office visit required more than just a clear head.

A quick pelvic exam by the abortion doctor revealed that I was not just six weeks pregnant, I was more like thirteen to fifteen weeks pregnant. With one hand raising my uterus, and his other hand on mine, the doctor and I stroked the length of a little fetus inside me. Then he brought out a fetal stethoscope, lubed it up, and stuck it on my belly. For the first time in my life, I heard the unmistakable, rapid whoosh, whoosh, whoosh of a baby's heartbeat. Jon looked at me, the doctor looked at Jon, the nurse looked at the doctor, and everybody wondered what the hell was going on. Jon has just realized that he wasn't responsible for this pregnancy, since we hadn't been together long enough. He was grinning. I was crying. I knew when it had happened.

In the den of our home, alone this time, I broke the news. I explained to my mother that, according to the new doctor, I was farther along than what our family doctor had estimated, and that I had some details to disclose. I was so scared. With only a little commotion, my mother retreated to a back bedroom phone to call my dad who was a big city police officer working the night shift—fighting crime and saving babies. I wish I could have listened in on that phone call: What was she making up? Or exaggerating, as she did? I did know that my siblings were eavesdropping from their bedrooms at the end of the hall.

Later that evening, my dad arrived in his navy blue Plymouth cruiser. He clanked and jingled with his uniform and belt gear on. I cringed when I heard him coming. He was nearly six and a half feet tall, and looked like Alan Alda. But that night, he was outraged: jaw-clenched, and mad as hell. For the next few hours I spilled my guts, so to speak. I explained how I had been running around with neighbors, bikers, and other Hell's Angels kind of nomads, and that I'd been hanging out with an older man over the summer that no one but my sister had known about. His name was Pasqual. He was a long, dark-haired, dark-eyed, Harley-riding, homeless outlaw from the bad side of the tracks. I had to call him my boyfriend, not only because it was safer among the circles he ran with, but because if my parents knew that he had tied me down with tent stakes and raped me in a field outside of Moriarty, New Mexico, my dad would probably have killed him. And not because he knocked-up his daughter, but because Pasqual was Mexican. I blamed myself for the rape. I wished that my dad would kill me instead.

As it was in 1977, the only hospital in the state that performed abortions past the thirteenth week was the county medical center in Albuquerque. With a two-week waiting period, my procedure date was set for the day before Thanksgiving. I was about sixteen to seventeen weeks into gestation. In the meantime, I attended high school, and tried to go on with my life. Too strange was the day before our school's Homecoming. I accompanied a girlfriend to a fancy dress shop in a nearby strip mall after class; I stepped into a dressing room and slid into a fancy amber-colored evening gown, just for the fun of it. In the three-sided mirror, I noticed my belly standing out there, in full view. I was a young woman in her second trimester of pregnancy. And I looked down at my full breasts, taking one then the other nipple into my fingers and squeezing. It was colostrum, the yellowish pre-nursing discharge that only mothers get. I did not see myself as a mother. I was turning sixteen in a couple of days.

The day before I was admitted to the hospital, I visited my new doctor's office where he placed a laminaria inside my cervix. A laminaria is a slow soaking, seaweed, a cervical expansion object. "This is the first of the invaders," I thought. The next day I awoke with an anxiety I cannot even explain. I sat in the tub and obsessed about my appearance. I hated my hair, my skin, my double chin. I thought of the laminaria stick in my cervix and I imagined it growing, widening the invader's highway. Never did I ask myself, however, "Why me?" But I did wonder what to do next. How I wished for someone to ask me how I was doing, what I was feeling, and did I perhaps need to talk. I did not lack company, but I needed comfort.

We must have looked like some kind of entourage as we checked into the hospital: my family, the mob. Here were the parents, and the Johnny-do-gooder-but-off-the-hook-boyfriend, and the soulless patient who checked in to deliver her body to the ultimate struggle between karma and consequence. One thing I was thankful for right away was the private room.

Without any sort of an orientation or introduction, I was stripped down to a gown and whisked across the hallway to a procedure room. It was here that I was, again, in the company of familiar faces: my doctor and his nurse, Juanita. He was wearing a pin-striped suit, he talked like a New Yorker, and had the nose of a Roman. She had permed hair and pink lips, and snuck cigarettes in a break room between patients.

As I looked straight ahead I heard his voice command me to reason and self-control. My legs were placed in stirrups and my right arm was strapped down while an intravenous tube was put in place. "Everybody's going to be cool here, okay?" He said it twice, while I looked up at the ceiling. In that instant I felt the pressure of several inches of needle, penetrating first my abdomen, muscle, tissue, and then my uterus. Some fluid was sucked out as the prostaglandin drug replaced it. "I wish it was me who was dying today," I thought to myself. In fact, I actually tried to. In those first few minutes, I stepped away from my self, my physical self; my soul-self stepped aside. This was the part of me that remembers seeing my body on the table, and the doctor directly above my face, calling for me to come back. "Come back!" he screamed at me. I would have left for good if I could have.

There are no words to describe the next four hours of painful uterine contractions. I did not have a clue about what was happening to my body. No one, not the doctor, his nurse, my mother, or anyone explained the dynamics of the process. I did not grasp what was happening or what would happen later. The less said, the better, I suppose they thought. I lay in the bed, writhing, miserable, wanting something to drink so desperately. And my mother stood at my bedside, firm and insisting that I "pull myself together." "Now you just stop this, right now. You just pull yourself together," she said.

My father looked forward. More than once, they reminded me that this was what happened to nice girls who don't come home on the weekends. My boyfriend stood there like some kind of hero with his hands in his pockets, bonding with my parents because none of them were as stupid as I was, the patient, writhing, sweat-soaked, slut-girl who had gotten what she deserved.

Only a few hours later, the amniotic fluid went everywhere. I was flabbergasted, and called for help, but soon apologized to the nurses when they came: "I'm sorry to bother you, but…so sorry, really to have made such a mess." My mother stood at her corner post, regaling us with how much she and I were alike because all of her "babies were born shortly after the onset of labor," and "by golly," I was going to be just like her. I thought she was crazy. I thought I was, too.

The next few hours got really crazy in my little one-bed, one-bath, two-chair private room. I wanted to walk, barf, sleep, breathe, but I couldn't do anything but writhe. The pain was unspeakable. I felt the need to use the bathroom when something started descending and my mother, who was trying to help me to the corner stall-style bathroom, kept forcing an orange bedpan underneath me. At one point, in desperation, I glanced between my legs, and I saw a head. It was dark and bluish, and seemed to have little dark hairs. In that split-second instant there was a nurse on the floor searching between my legs. She was in a bit of a panic herself, fumbling with gloves and clamps, then whisking away the bedpan contents.

It wasn't even over by midnight, when I had to walk back across the hall to the dreaded procedure room for a D&C (Dilation and Curettage), because the placenta had not detached, and they needed to go in and scrape it out. I said goodnight to my dad and my boyfriend, and to my mother, who looked at me as if to ask "What's next?" She leaned into my ear and whispered "What a gem that Jon is—now you be good to him, he's a keeper. We'll see you tomorrow."

The next day was Thanksgiving Day. Following my release, I rushed home to put on some tight-fitting jeans so as to exhibit my former self. They were so very tight, but I made myself wear them, and made myself act normal and friendly amidst my extended family. I tried hard to integrate back into society on this day after. The oversized Kotex pad between my legs was cumbersome and was a continual reminder of what had just happened. That day my mother must have felt some sense of sympathy for me because, from time to time, in between her cooking and serving, she would sneak me drags off of her Virginia Slims cigarettes, or slide me a couple of Valium. And then, of course, on these special occasions, I did get to have a drink or two, or six.

It took me a long time to get to a place where I could talk about that experience, but I'm done crying about it. I'm done moralizing and rationalizing about it. For many years I put on a big brave smile, even through two more early-term abortions. I have long wanted to tell this story. What matters most, I suppose, is my need to believe I can tell the story without shame. I did the research, and have resigned from further human and spiritual devaluation of myself by finding strength not only in my claim to feminist ideology, but through my spiritual growth as well. I have come to terms with my unplanned pregnancies and I accept the experience as an exercise in relationship dynamics, and in karmic and spiritual soul lessons. In time I have come to see how everybody involved in that experience had a role, a job to do, and something to learn. I do not hate my parents for their absence of education. And I know they were scared. Over time, I have become comfortable with the claim that what I aborted is what I say it is, and not dictated by the authority of some outside moral authority, be it the church or the law.

What I experienced was unique to me in my evolving self. To me, it was not an act of murder, as the religious zealots and right wing oppressors would condemn, because I believe the soul and the personality (which includes the body) are separate energies. I believe that we can check in and out of our physical vehicles when the situation requires it—or desires it. And I think that in cases where a woman chooses to terminate her pregnancy, there is an agreement between her soul-self and that of her child. There is always agreement.

Compassion is the gift of grief. I am a wise, compassionate, and understanding person as a consequence of having walked through that pain. I have come to realize that it's too important to not speak up—my silence does not protect me.

How can I forget this when nearly every day my visible reminder is a little white scar on my right hand, left by an intravenous needle from more than twenty years ago? I see it often: when I am driving, when my hand is at rest on the keyboard, and when I apply lotion. To me, it is a symbol of the critical need for education. Young women, and men, must have access to information about drugs, alcohol, anatomy, their sense of self, birth control, abstinence, self-esteem, making choices, and seeing the future for themselves. My great regret is that I just simply did not think about the choices I made. My choices put me in situations that compromised my integrity. I did not know any better.

More than anything, I wish somebody had educated me before any of this happened. Somebody should have talked to me and my friends about our bodies, our ideas, our very lives. I wish I'd had more self-confidence so that I could have resisted flattering enticements, lures, and male seduction.

We need to be talking to little girls about what some men will do, say, and expect. We should be talking to our kids about healthy human sexuality and how to love, respect, and choose for ourselves.

In this, our time, I call upon all women everywhere to awaken their power, to find themselves, and to speak their truth. For some, breaking the silence and telling the truth about the past is a creative act, rich with symbolic possibilities and full of potential for self-discovery and transformation. For me, my truths and all of my experiences, good and bad, constitute the person I am today.

At the end of the day, and the end of this paper, my only regret is that I didn't say it sooner.

I ONLY CALL WOMEN

Avra*

I exclude. I exclude in a way that is not consciously intended, but which I lack the strength to avoid. I only call women.

It is only women who come to mind, only women whom I expect to empathize, to share my pain and anger until the distant day when those feelings begin to heal and dissipate.

I only call women, so only women can respond. Anna comes with me. She is my closest friend: her presence seems most necessary.

It is the absence, though, which is glaringly, maddeningly obvious. Andy is not there, does not come. Andy, the only one who must be there, whose presence and support I need in an overwhelming, inexplicable way. He cannot share, will not take his rightful part in this experience, and since he rarely leaves my thoughts, it is to him that I return as the prototype of all the men in my life, the men who matter most. His response has spoken for all of them in this stressful week.

No more pain, sirs, no more pain caused by men. You get no more opportunities to detach yourselves. I only call women.

In the waiting room, I think about which time it was. Not the first time. That was nice. Surprisingly nice, considering I felt pressured into it. We had no contraception.

Afterwards, I clung to him. Sex was still pretty new to me. At age eighteen, I always clung. "If only I'd known," he laughed. "If only I'd known a little sex would make you so romantic, I'd have done this a long time ago!"

It seemed like an adorable thing to say. Only a small part of me noticed the strange use of the pronoun "I." Didn't he mean "we?" But then he said, "I think I could fall in love with you." I fell asleep, content.

Luckily, my period came a week later. "I don't mind blood," he joked. "I'm going to be a doctor." So I put in my diaphragm and went to him.

Yet soon we saw the diaphragm could not suit our hurried trysts, in my cabin or his tent, on our brief free periods away from the campers. The diaphragm was too unwieldy, with its applicators and creams and apparatus. At least the rubber could fit in Andy's pocket.

Maybe it was the time the rubber broke. I didn't even notice until he stopped for a second and flung it off. "It ripped a couple of minutes ago," he muttered, annoyed. What?! But we kept going.

How could I? Why did I? All I can recall is a surge of desperation, a no-time-to-stop, it's-probably-too-late-anyway bombardment of passion, words, and rhythm. "I love you," he said. "I love you." He said it so many times that summer, but what could he have meant? Perhaps 'I love you, but ask for nothing, because that's all I have to give. Any show of concreteness must be kept for myself.'

I probably suspected it, as I heard his ambivalence in comments like, "I don't want my friends to know I love you," or "it's not you I'm running from, it's this suffocating relationship." Later, even harsher: "I'm a bastard. Why do you like me so much? Why don't you like one of the other counselors? They're all good-looking." Words to weight against: "If you get pregnant, I'll be there. Don't worry, sweetheart, you're probably not. But if you are, I'll pay for it. We're in this together. Remember that."

A week later: Positive test. I cry. He holds me. Loosely. "Andy," I say, trying to steady my voice. "I don't want you to use the fear that you feel as an excuse to end this relationship. This is going to be a really hard time for us, and we need each other." Sounds better than 'I need you,' I figure.

"It will all be okay," he answers, weakly.

"I love you so much," I say.

"I know," he nods brusquely. "You shouldn't have made the clinic appointment for Saturday. I'm busy this weekend."

So Hell is renewed in me. Saturday comes. Anna comes. Soon it is over, all over, and he is still gone. If only I could abort him and cast him out from inside me, maybe I would let the fetus stay. It could hardly occupy more space or cause more trouble than Andy already does. And yet I cannot expel him from my thoughts. I can only disavow his behavior. Instead, I find myself mimicking him. I shield myself from potentially painful situations.

I only call women.

*Editor's Note: The author has withheld her last name to protect her privacy.

SURPRISE (OR EVERYTHING TO DO WITH HOPE)

Rhonda Chittenden

For all the women and men who, caught unaware, rain harsh judgments upon themselves when the unexpected manifests itself in their communities, their clinics, their families, their relationships, their wombs.

Contrary to popular belief, Surprise did not creep in through a crack in the foundation on a dark, moonless night. Instead, it entered through an open window in the sun room one breezy afternoon. Gauzy curtains billowing, Surprise blew silently past me and settled in, waiting patiently for the right time to announce itself. When it finally did, I blamed myself for its presence. "I should have closed the window! I should have been better prepared! I was so naïve in thinking you'd never come!" Unfettered by my ranting, Surprise gathered tissue and blankets and made me a cup of herbal tea. Smoothing out a comfortable space for me to rest, Surprise said, "Your lack of preparation for my arrival is a complicated matter. Perhaps you could have anticipated it and made efforts to barricade yourself against me. But, at some point, you would become vulnerable." This did not console me. Surprise continued, "Vulnerability is not your fault. It is the human condition." I was quiet for a long time, but eventually began a conversation with Surprise that lasted for days. In the end I realized that, in spite of any efforts to control its access, Surprise will again enter my life. And although uninvited, Surprise never comes empty handed. Along with the initial upset, it also brings new insight and increased strength for those willing to accept its gifts. Rather than wasting energy in self-blame, I can experience Surprise as the Unexpected unfolding in my life. Beyond that, I realize Surprise is a reflection of my human innocence, a quality that has little to do with naivete and everything to do with hope.

THOUGHTS DURING MY ABORTION

Kathleen George Kearnery

"In its simplest construction, the abortion decision centers on the self. The concern is pragmatic and the issue is survival."[8]

I have come here to find meaning in scarlet
and salvation in ridding myself of it.
    Are you comfortable with your decision?
Yesterday I gulped holy water from a baptismal font
(when the priest wasn't looking, of course)
to find out if it would scorch.
And it didn't.
there, in the drafty narthex
I was laughing bitterly
had Mary herself considered abortion?
Wouldn't she, if only for a moment,
have resisted the angel,
made the angel turn on a furious golden heel?
    Try to relax. You can hold my hand if you like.
There are noises no saint ever told me about.
And I hold the saints responsible, I do.
No saint Christopher or Theresa ever explained to me
that there are nights and beds and men with rage
that even God can't reach.
God didn't reach for me then, as I cried and pulled at the sheets,
and I won't let God reach me now.
Only this doctor can reach me,
and this counselor with her hardened eyes,
and the girl who sat next to me in the waiting room—

        she's just a baby herself, Lord.
I can barely hear the protesters screaming now:
they lie to women in there they only want your money come and talk to us we care about you this doctor hurts women when you have your ultrasound make them turn the screen so you can look at your baby you'll see how beautiful and happy your baby is—
something lurches inside me,
I am too afraid to ask what it is, but the voice comes down smooth and calm:
       try to focus for one more minute. You're almost through
dreams pound against my hollow breathing,
yelling prayer into the abyss,
imagining the pieces of vows made to the Church,
now broken open and out and up,
now left behind when I choose my own vows.
Eyes close, and there is Jesus,
Jesus watching. I have never seen him watching before.
       Try to think of something else.
My mother comes to mind. That's no good.
Sensation of something running out of me—
my faith, or the contents of my uterus?
My mother cried when I was born, when I skinned my knee at five,
when I decided to go to a liberal arts college,
when I told her I didn't think the Rapture would happen any time soon.
And I wonder what my mother is doing now.
The sound of scraping.
Mary is washing her son's wounds. He is dead,
but it doesn't matter.
I grip the tough hands of the counselor.
My mother is washing dishes in her dull yellow kitchen,

each time she dips a pot into the soapy water,
it comes out scarlet. She pauses, perhaps
is even in awe for one brief moment, for the first time in her life,
but doesn't stop washing.
PLEASE DON'T KILL YOUR DAUGHTER,
chant the picketers over and over.
I crack my eyes, hope to see a chalice, a stained glass window,
a watchful baptismal font.
       I am still thirsty.
The doctor is bent over, her wispy hair hiding her face.
Something dangles off her neck—is it my soul,
plunging from the pin that the angels dance on?
It glitters and swings.
Confused sunlight plays.
I think I spy Jesus.
Her cross moves outside the rhythm of the chanting.
Resurrections are never easy,
and never mundane.

I slip,
and I pull for red
and I slide through.

SILENCE

Jennifer Powis

You know, it wasn't even me but I felt like it was. The circumstances were unreal; I almost think you won't believe them but I need to talk about it, to explain, to no one in particular.

We were participating in a Summer-at-Sea program. Living on a boat for three months, taking classes and washing dishes. I was from Ohio and she was from Texas. By chance, or luck, we were roommates and became friends. But by July, she knew she was pregnant, alone and eighteen, and pregnant on a boat in the middle of the Caribbean Sea.

She was scared, but more importantly, she was alone with me, a naïve lesbian. I had no idea what she could do, how she could do it, but we both knew she needed an abortion. At port on the next island, she begged me to come with her, to hold her hand, to listen and see. We went to a tourist information booth, where I stood outside as a lookout while she opened her heart to the women who worked there. I remember walking back in, seeing her crying on a shoulder covered in crazy colored cloth. I remember these women holding her, as if she were a daughter, and reassuring her that "this Western doctor" was good. He was safe and clean—things I hadn't even thought about yet. But me, who was I to think about them? It was her decision and I was her support. We had only known each other for a month.

I don't know if I was much help. Probably not. But I do know that I wanted to talk about it and, for some reason, I couldn't. I'm not even sure we ever said the word "abortion" between the two of us. That is the profound truth. Even while we were searching for a doctor, crying, walking; even while we were alone, we never said that word: abortion. As if this situation would be different as long as we never said it out loud. Needless to say, the silence between us was audible.

The doctor was clean. The doctor was not very nice. She borrowed my money, and spent all of hers. And I haven't seen her since. The quiet, though, is what still haunts me. The fact that we never talked about it. But then I try to think of what I would have said, or how I would have said it. Really, at age eighteen, what did I know of the world? Although I admit I thought I knew everything. This two-hour process took me by surprise and wrapped the guilt of silence around me. I couldn't speak because she couldn't. It wasn't guilt, it wasn't fear, it was innocence. What was there to say?

MULTIPLE CHOICE

Katherine M. DePasquale

Around the age of nine or ten, my mother started accusing me of being pregnant on a regular basis. I'd come home from school and she'd tell me I was a whore and a slut, and that she knew I was either pregnant or was soon going to be. I remember always being afraid that maybe I *was* pregnant, since I didn't know how one became pregnant in the first place. The only thing I knew for sure was that being pregnant was a very bad thing.

I never wanted to abuse my own children; I also remember thinking, at age sixteen, that being pregnant would end any hopes of going to college. I had managed to escape from my mother and, at the time, was living on my own with whoever would take me in (sometimes in shelters) which forced me to drop out of high school.

I am in my thirties now. I got a G.E.D (General Equivalency Diploma) when I was twenty and graduated from college *Phi Beta Kappa* in 1996. And, to this day, I am deathly afraid of pregnancy. The bottom line is that the older I get, the less I want children. I sometimes have nightmares that I have given birth without knowing I was even pregnant, or that I've become pregnant and am alone. It all sounds pretty bizarre, I suppose, but I think some of this fear is rational under the circumstances. But what does this have to do with reproductive choice?

I am simultaneously the pro-choice movement's worst-case scenario and the *anti*-choice movement's best public relations gimmick: a woman who has had multiple abortions (three). I am that theoretical woman who is so sexually irresponsible that, despite all education, help, guidance, and wisdom to the contrary, she becomes pregnant again and again. Right?

When I was sixteen, I entered into a four-year relationship with a partner who was HIV positive. This should have made us doubly cautious; we should, if anything, have used two condoms at all times. In fact, we rarely used any condoms. To this day, when I look back on my behavior, I can't honestly say that I understand why we didn't. We knew we were supposed to be using condoms, but instead chose to use that highly acclaimed birth control method known as "withdrawal." This actually went pretty well for three years; I guess we just got lucky. In the space of six months, though, when I was nineteen, I became pregnant twice, and had two abortions. I chalked it all up to the fact that I'd quit smoking and was, therefore, more fertile. I started smoking again and, when our relationship ended, just counted my blessings that despite four years of unprotected sex, I was—and remain—HIV negative.

By the time I got pregnant for the third time, I was in my mid-twenties, but this time it was just a mistake in my calculations, pure and simple. In my quest for alternative birth control I chose the sympto-thermal method. This method is probably more suitable for a couple who wishes to avoid pregnancy, but wouldn't mind if it happened. It relies on daily temperature readings and bodily observations, but I simplified the whole thing into a thirty day counting method. One month of that earned me my last unwanted pregnancy.

I'm not proud of making the same mistake over and over; I wish I'd been more careful. But the pressure to keep silent about my abortion experiences is suffocating. I elected to undergo a medical procedure that is legal in this country, but yet there are very few people to whom it can be "safely" mentioned. I know because I tell a lot of people, and I see their reactions. Sometimes, someone will mention a particularly annoying aspect of pregnancy, such as "morning" sickness (it actually lasted all day for me), and I'll say, "I know what you mean!" Or someone who is particularly insistent that I reproduce forces it out of me (usually men) saying, "Oh, all women want babies…just wait a few years; you'll see."

I don't think my story is typical, and I know that the majority of women and girls who seek abortions are not "repeat offenders." But the anti-choice movement would have you believe that women like me "get what they deserve." Even some pro-choice folks are more sympathetic to a rape or incest survivor who needs an abortion. Of course, this is natural; in addition to the traumas rape and incest survivors experience, they are the women who are most likely to be hurt by anti-abortion laws. But I needed access to abortion, too. I don't just *think* that I wouldn't have gotten my G.E.D. and graduated from college were it not for my ability to choose an abortion, I know it.

I want people to understand that I am not irresponsible, and that I did not undertake my abortions lightly. They were extremely stressful, but they were, for me, the best decisions. For people who view abortion as murder and a zygote or embryo as a baby, nothing I say will change their mind. The fact that their focus is so obviously an issue of control over women's bodies precludes any rational discourse on the topic. The problem, though, is that the anti-abortion people have informed abortion discourse so strongly in America that we are actually unable to discuss these experiences *in any form, with anyone.* And I do not just think that such discussions would have prevented my own pregnancies and abortions, I know it.

HURRICANES AND OTHER BACKLASH

Kristy Beckman, age 17

Every time
It hits like a whirlwind
I try to keep my cool.
Calm. Collected. Focused.
I know what's right;
The rest shouldn't matter...
But my reasoning stops here.
I've run head-on
Into a brick wall.

They're picketing my high school!
Pictures of blown up fetuses
So raw it turns your gut.
Later we found out
Some of the photos were really miscarriages.
They tell the young womyn who were raped
(And all the young womyn who will be raped)
That it's their own fault.
Apparently you can *make* someone rape you these days.

A car whirs by,
Its bumper sticker stating,
"Pro-Life
Your name's a lie;
You don't care if womyn die!"
A victory
Making me tremble with even more fear

Of these picketers who don't give a damn
About me (us)

Later, after school
Tallying surveys about "sexual" assault
Half of the 16-, 17-, and 18-year-old womyn
Believe they won't get pregnant
If he pulls out.
(But he can't really control his behavior,
by the way,
So you're still at fault when this fails.)
They're not arming us with knowledge;
They're filling us with a sickly, creeping fear.

The next day, in Health
We are lectured on erections, ejaculations, and wet dreams.
A diagram of the female anatomy
Is handed out
Suspiciously, the clitoris and labia are missing…
Because we are SLUTS if we desire.
We can only *be* desired.
He gets passion, you get pregnant.

I'm dragged to church
(Where "He" has a capital "H")
The priest reminds me:
Birth control is a sin!
Pleasure is a sin!
Oh, yeah…Womyn are sin!

My friend calls me that night.
"I'm pregnant," she whispers.

"…No, I'm not afraid of the abortion…
But I'm terrified of the protesters!"
She bursts into sobs
"Will you come with me?
…What? My boyfriend?
He broke it off. He thinks abortion should be banned,
Not that he wants to be a father."

Then a phone call *about* a friend.
Her dad got her pregnant.
The judge told her to get his permission
To terminate her pregnancy.
Because she was too afraid
To tell her story
A guy she knew tried to do it.
So sorry. Bled to death.

"THEY'RE KILLING US!"
I hope the scream wasn't only inside my head;
Someone else has got to notice.
And the whirlwind's not over yet.

TIPPED UTERUS

Toni Presti

When I was fifteen, that's the tenth grade, I got pregnant. My boyfriend was twenty years old, and we were using the "pull out" method of contraception. I could not make the phone call for the abortion from my house, because it was a secret. So I had to do it at school. I remember going to school that day with about five dollars worth of change weighing down my jeans. Calls were ten cents back then. I cut my first class, biology, and I went to a pay phone underneath a stairwell. I had my list of abortion clinics, and I went down the list until I found one that would take patients on a Saturday. So I arranged to meet my boyfriend on the corner where we all hung out. He was twenty minutes late. By the time he got there, my semi-adult composure went right out the window.

We drove to the clinic. We went up to the reception area and Matthew paid the $135, and the nurse said it would be another fifty dollars for anesthesia. We didn't know about that, and we didn't have another fifty dollars. But, at the time, I didn't really know what anesthesia was. So, I said, "That's alright. Forget it. I don't need that." Next, I went into the operating room and there was a nurse in there prepping the room. She was a big, solid, Black woman about sixty years old. She began to prep both me and the room with this sort of rhythm. And she took me in and lulled me with it. She talked about her daughter's garden: Marigolds. Then the doctor came in. He looked between my legs and smiled. He looked at my face and he smiled. Then he flipped on the machine and he smiled.

Afterwards, I went into the recovery room. It was a big room; unsupervised, filled with young women crying and sort of yelling and walking around. I sat in a green lazyboy chair, quiet. Rigid. About five minutes later a girl came in and sat down in a twin lazyboy chair next to mine. She was beautiful, and I remember feeling so awkward and ugly because she was so gorgeous. All of a sudden she grabbed my hand and just held it really tight, and she looked at me. When I think about it now, I realize I fell in love, right there. She was crying and she said, "It hurts."

And then she fell asleep with my hand. I wanted to get out of that room so badly, but I didn't want to let go of her. I did, though. I untangled myself, and I left.

The thing about it is, whenever the subject of abortion comes up, when I hear it from a friend or on the news, or whatever, I feel a tug, and I realize it's her. It's that girl holding my hand.

THAT WAS A VERY GOOD YEAR

Marie King[*]

My abortion experience occurred while I was in the Army, stationed at Fort Gordon, Georgia. Born and raised in the northern part of Michigan, I joined the military at the age of twenty-six.

As a fallen-away Catholic, I did not attend church, but still felt the pull of the Church's teachings. Although I was sexually active, I did not use birth control because I thought it would "officially" make me a sinner, ignoring the fact that being sexually active was also against my religion.

I had several partners, but felt I was "in love" with Bobbie, who was Black and several years my senior. We had met one night when I walked by the television room in the barracks, and he jumped out and asked me to go to a carnival with him. I refused at first, but he finally wore me down and I agreed to go.

He was married, which I did not know at the time since his wife was stationed at another military base. After our first date, he continued to pursue me, and we eventually ended up having sex on several occasions. Eventually, his interest in me waned, but I was still very much interested in him. It was an exciting and dangerous experience for me for a couple of reasons.

One reason was because of our different races. I had not been exposed to people from diverse backgrounds until I had joined the Army. The town in which I grew up was completely White, except for a couple of college students. I had no opinion one way or the other about Black people. The only time I had ever really thought about them was during the race riots in Detroit in 1968 when people in my town began to panic, thinking that angry Black people were going to come up, by the busloads, to destroy my community. I was only about twelve years old, so I got scared because the adults were scared. Now when I look back on it, I see what a sad situation it was.

It felt dangerous and exciting for another reason: our difference in rank. He was an E-6, a "non-commissioned officer," while I was an E-3, fresh out of signal school. The Army does not allow fraternization between non-commissioned officers (NCOs) and junior enlisted members. There is also a very strict policy against dating a married person. If we had been caught, we both would have faced very serious charges.

When I found out I was pregnant, I made the decision almost immediately that I would get an abortion. I did not consult anyone, since there was no one to consult. Bobbie was not interested, and, as I said, we could have gotten into a great deal of trouble for having had a relationship, so I couldn't go to anyone in my company. As strict Catholics, my family would not have been any help to me; instead they would have condemned me for getting pregnant and, additionally, for getting pregnant with a Black man. I had no friends with whom I felt comfortable talking about the pregnancy, so I called Planned Parenthood in Augusta to schedule an appointment for an abortion.

Since my appointment was scheduled for a Friday, I needed to request a day off. When I went to talk to my immediate supervisor, Jaime, he observed that something was upsetting me. I broke down and told him the situation after making him swear that he would not tell anyone. He and I had an excellent relationship, so I knew I could trust him. Then he asked me what I was going to do after the procedure was over, and I told him that I was planning to come back to the barracks. He offered me the option of staying with him and his wife over the weekend, which I decided to do.

When I arrived at Planned Parenthood on the morning of my appointment, they counseled me and did some blood tests; then I went into the procedure room and met the doctor. I laid down on the table and while he was doing the procedure, a nurse stood next to me and held my hand. I squeezed her hand so tight, I'm afraid I left nail marks. It felt like it was never going to end. I gritted my teeth and held her hand until it was over. Then I went to the recovery room.

As I closed my eyes and put my head back against the chair, I noticed for the first time that the radio was playing a song I'll never forget: "When I was seventeen, that was a very good year..." It was the first time I cried during the whole experience. Up until then, I had been able to keep my emotions buried, but the song made me think about lost innocence and how I had just lost mine.

I also felt terrible for the child that was not going to be. I had decided against adoption because I was afraid that the baby would be mistreated because it would be a "mixed" child living in the deep south. I had been told that the Klan had its headquarters in Augusta, just doors away from the Planned Parenthood clinic.

After I left the clinic, I went to Jaime's house to spend the weekend. I spent most of the time on the couch because I was so physically weak. I think I was somewhat in shock, not fully able to believe I had done such a thing. I wanted to get up and resume my normal life, but I couldn't. My body needed time to recover and my emotions were jumping all over the place. Jaime and his wife were there for me when I had no one to turn to. I feel eternally grateful to them. Unfortunately, I've lost contact with them. I just wish they knew how much it meant to me that they took care of me when I was alone.

Sunday evening, I went back to my room in the barracks. I walked down to the kitchen to make something to eat and Bobbie was in the hallway buffing the floor. He followed me into the kitchen, telling me how worried he had been when I hadn't shown up in the barracks Friday night. His only reaction, when I told him where I had been, was to groan, "Now he (Jaime) knows about this?" The fact that Jaime knew seemed to cause him a great deal of distress. I took delight in his discomfort because he had been such a jerk throughout the whole ordeal.

On Monday morning, I had to join the company run because I had no medical excuse from the Army. When I went into the shower after the run, my vision disappeared: I couldn't see anything. I felt my way back to my room and sat down on the bed, and slowly my vision returned. I decided I had better go on "sick call" so that I could be excused from duty for the day. I made it to the medical clinic and started to faint, so they rushed me to a gurney. The medic who took my blood pressure got a very worried look on his face and said that I needed to be transported to the hospital. When I got to the hospital, they sent me to the Obstetrics and Gynecology clinic, where I waited for two hours. When I finally saw a doctor, he ordered a pregnancy test and gave me an medical excuse from duty for the rest of the day. By this time it was early afternoon, so I went back to my room to lie down. That was the extent of my sick time.

Later that week, I finally worked up the courage to call one of my friends to tell her about the abortion. She was shocked, I think, but she listened while I told her the whole story and then she tried to make me feel better. I was glad I had finally talked to someone, especially someone who really knew me.

I spent the next month crying my eyes out, then the Army transferred me to Texas. Once I got away from Georgia, the pain eased up somewhat, but not the guilt. Then I was sent to Germany, where I met my husband. He had been in the military for quite a while and had encountered all types of situations, so he took it in stride when I told him about the abortion.

After we were married, the abortion continued to bother me, so I went to the Catholic priest on my military post and told him what I had done. He was good to me; he told me that because God forgave me, I too should forgive myself. It has taken me quite a while, but I am finally at peace. With the exception of this kindly priest, Jaime, my husband, and my friend, I have told no one about the choice I made. Recently, my friend told me that she thought I did the right thing and that she probably would have done the same thing if she were in a similar situation.

Now, I have two beautiful sons, who I am thankful for every day. Although I have forgiven myself, I would never have another abortion. But I think that abortion should be available to those who need it. The individual woman is the person who has to live with herself, so she is the only one who can make the decision to have, or to not have, an abortion.

*Editor's Note: The author has used a pseudonym to protect her privacy.

A TRIP TO HELL (AT AGE FOURTEEN)

Mary Grant*

I remember feeling frightened the minute Rob passed by my street when he was supposed to be taking me home. I had the fleeting thought that I might be embarking on an adventure. Thus far I had lived a life of protected naivete; now I was excited to be doing something "wrong." Besides, Rob was a friend of my boyfriend Tommy's, and it was Tommy who had asked Rob to take me home, so I assumed he wouldn't do anything to actually hurt me. I figured, worse comes to worst, he would only try kissing me, and *then* take me home.

I started to converse with Rob as if everything were normal. He returned the conversation. I wanted so much to be liked that I refused to think of anything else but how nice it was to have the company of this older (he was eighteen years old), cute, new friend. I ignored the fact that he had already betrayed my trust. I ignored some rumors I'd heard about him possibly being involved with drugs—mainly because he was a friend of my boyfriend's, who was a god to me. I didn't even think about the fact that the pizzeria he worked at, which was owned and run by his family, had been investigated by the police. I didn't want to think this guy was bad. That would mean being frightened and vulnerable. I wanted to feel adventurous, sophisticated, in-the-know about life, perfectly capable of handling myself with an older guy. I wanted to trust him and I wanted him to think I was pretty. I thought, for sure, that he was taking me somewhere to tell me he'd been watching, with envy, all these months that I'd been dating Tommy. That he wanted to be my boyfriend. I wanted to believe so many sweet, naïve things.

When we got to his house, I think I met his brother (much of what happened is pretty fuzzy). I realized that I had seen his brother before. I was surprised that they were brothers, since they didn't look at all alike; possibly they were stepbrothers. I knew his mom was dating the guy she ran the pizzeria with. This was something new and exciting to me, since I came from an intact family. Their house was different than mine: it was starkly furnished, and what my mother would call "white-trashy." And because their way of living was different from mine, to me that meant *better*.

He brought me down to his basement. It was a furnished basement that was actually his own "pad" (his word). He lived there rather independently. His mom didn't ask questions, he told me, and didn't pry into his life. As I was getting accustomed to this small space with no natural light, he asked me if I was thirsty.

This seemed a normal, polite thing to do, so I said yes. He went back upstairs. He did not return for a while so I went up the basement steps and found the door locked. He opened it just as I was retreating. I explained away the locked door in my fantasy-mind as him trying to protect me from something *he* knew about and I didn't—what a nice guy! I felt ashamed when he caught me trying to open the door! As he came down the stairs he told me he always locked the door out of habit. After all, it was *his* room. I understood immediately. I had three siblings and *wished* I could have some privacy at home.

Around this point I began to be concerned about the time. Earlier, when all this had begun, he'd put my bike in his trunk and started to drive me home because it was raining and I needed to get home. Now, it was getting very late. My parents would be pissed. I told him I had to be home for dinner. He said not to worry. He'd get me home in time. He handed me the glass of iced tea he had just got from the kitchen. It was a big glass and before I was halfway through it I was feeling woozy and dizzy. I told him something seemed weird. I wasn't feeling right. I asked (jokingly, though feeling a rising fear) what he put in the drink. He responded, "Nothing. Relax."

We made small talk. I was quickly losing my faculties but trying with all my might to remain "normal" and clear-headed. I saw a long line of mirrors under a glass bookshelf where his stereo was and asked him about them. He asked me if I'd ever done coke. I said I'd drunk it before but that I didn't like soda. I thought maybe he didn't hear my question about the mirrors or that perhaps I was confusing things. So I asked what he meant by the coke question. He showed me a long line of white powder on a mirror, took a straw and sniffed the stuff up his nose! Then he asked me if I wanted any! "No!" I said, "I could never put anything up my nose!" He laughed at me and mentioned something about a lot of people doing it and that he made a lot of money because of it. I didn't understand what he was talking about. Actually, I couldn't understand much at this point.

He then brought out this big glass pipe-like thing with a bubble at the base of it and he asked me if I knew what it was. I said, "No." He took a lighter and lit something and there was suddenly a whole bunch of smoke in the glass. He put his face to it and took a breath in. He smiled. Then he forced my head onto it! It covered both my nose *and* mouth! I tried to hold my breath so I wouldn't breathe in the smoke, but he held my head for what seemed like five minutes. Finally I *had* to breathe. I took a huge gulp of the smoke and thought I was going to die. It hurt my lungs something awful. I was panicking now, and I'm sure my eyes were bulging. The room was spinning and I couldn't hold my head up.

I got from the couch to his bed as if by magic. He must have carried me or thrown me; I don't know. Once on the bed, "it" started for real. He started taking my shirt off. I was so ashamed of my body—I never let anyone see my skin if I could help it—that I tried to hold my clothes on as he was ripping them off. I wanted him to stop. I protested with all the strength I could muster but my guess is that I barely made any sense. I couldn't think clearly. At some point I must have whined because he hit me.

I cried. I said I wanted to go home. He hit me again, and told me I was gonna "do it" with him. Today. Now. I think he called me a cock-tease. I didn't know what that meant, but it sounded mean and not how I thought of myself. Then, he stopped abruptly and started convincing me that everything was "cool" and that this was good. "This is what people who are in love do," he told me. I thought that he meant that he loved me, so I asked him, "Do you love me?" He hit me again and laughed. I tried to make sense of things, but it was a losing battle. Between the drugs and my fears (and trying to *squash* my fears and deal with the situation) and the contradictory things he was saying, I couldn't keep track or understand anymore.

Then he penetrated me. I was shocked! I didn't know what was happening, but I did not expect *this*! I cried out and he hit me. He said people upstairs would hear me if I didn't shut up. I cried out again and said that it hurt. I tried to reason with him. He kept ramming his penis into me and smacking my face. His penis was too large for my vagina. I had no reference for what was happening and remember thinking about the one time I had seen a penis before. My brother or a cousin peed outside and I saw it (We were very young at the time). I thought that was all a guy did with that "thing." I thought he was really strange for putting it inside the place I peed from! I wondered if anyone else had ever done this. Probably not, I figured, because it hurt too much! Must just be something mean people, like him, do. These thoughts were all very fleeting. I would have a moment or two of clear thinking and then I'd slip back into oblivion. He ripped some of my clothes and all I could think was that my parents were going to be really pissed off at me. I guess I shut down: mentally, emotionally, or both. I decided this horrible thing wasn't really happening to me.

Then I began to pretend that we were in love. This act seemed so intimate, I'd never been so *close* to another person before. I pretended that it didn't hurt. I think I even left my body at one point, because I remember seeing us "down there" together in a strange, gyrating image of mingling bodies and weird sounds.

I must have fallen asleep or passed out because I remember waking up and immediately panicking that I had to get home immediately. My parents terrified me at that point in my life, probably more than this guy, or being raped, did. I was so afraid of what my father would do: hit me or worse—not like or love me anymore. Most likely he'd be disappointed in me. I started to speak really fast in a high-pitched voice, saying that I had to get home, and Rob hit me again. He told me to calm down and call my parents. I told him I couldn't, that I was too groggy and couldn't think straight enough to fool them. He came up with some lie for me to tell them.

At that point it became "us against them." I was now, somehow, a partner with this guy in the terrible thing he had just done to me. So now, it just couldn't be terrible anymore. It had to be something I chose to do, so that I could feel comfortable with lying about it. Rob helped me. He acted as though this was a normal thing to lie about. Like when my girlfriend and I would "hang out" in places where we weren't allowed to, and then we'd lie to our parents. The rape was being reduced to something of that magnitude.

Right after I hung up with my father, who was very angry, I talked to Rob like he was a friend, again. I told him how afraid I was of my father. How my mother was even worse. I went to him for comfort! I curled up with him and he took it to mean I wanted more sex and the whole thing started all over again! I tried to protest and realized that he always hit me when I did that, so I started to think about whether or not I could actually enjoy it. Or pretend I did. I found that I could, if I just concentrated on my physical, tactile senses. My body was now doing something it was naturally meant to do, so of course it felt good. Talk about messing with a girl's head, though! This, I think, was what clamped the lid on the case: I felt certifiably bad and slutty for years after because I learned to enjoy sex during a rape. Who but a true whore would enjoy being raped? It would be years before I was able even to think about the event long enough to realize exactly what I found enjoyable at that moment: it was the natural, physical sensations, not the rape itself.

A song came on the radio at some point and he said it was "our song." Teenage girls are always thinking how this or that song fits how they feel about a guy. Now, this guy was doing that with a song, dedicating it to me, and it was about "true love" and being "the only one"—another mixed, painful message. I started to romanticize him and our "relationship," at the same time I swore that I'd forever hate that song.

Not long after the song I pulled myself together enough to ask him to take me home. He said no at first. I panicked again. I knew that if he didn't take me home, I'd never get there. I had no idea where I was, and we'd driven much farther from my house than I'd ever gone before. (It turned out to be about twenty miles away—an impossible distance for a kid with no transportation.) He finally agreed to drive me home, but he laughed and teased me, calling me a baby and taunting me about not being able to find my own way home. I was humiliated by this, on top of everything else.

On the drive back, at first I sat at the far side of the front seat, by the window. He commented that I was a "fraidy-cat" and that he wouldn't hurt me so I moved closer (I was quietly afraid he would hurt me if I didn't). Then I cuddled with him! I wanted so much to be comforted at this point, loved and cared for. In my head I kept flipping between two futures: in one I would make it home and forget everything that happened and life would go on like it had before (not a happy prospect, really); in the other I would marry him and we'd live "happily ever after." Of course we would date first, but move to marriage quickly because we were so much "in love."

He then made a comment about my virginity. I didn't understand. The only time I'd heard the word "virgin" was in reference to the Virgin Mary. I couldn't relate anything to that, so I asked him what he meant. He laughed at me and said it meant that I had never "done it" before. I still didn't understand. He said it meant I'd never had sex before. I said I wasn't going to have sex until I was married. He looked at me really strange and said, "You idiot! You just had sex!"

I was devastated. I hadn't realized, even at that point, what had really happened. I started thinking about God and what I had learned in church and on the television, and said, "Well, then, we have to get married." He laughed hard at that. I continued, "What if I'm pregnant now? Would you marry me if I'm pregnant?" I had heard that when you had sex, you got pregnant. I didn't know any particulars, but I trusted that this guy was telling me the truth—that we'd had sex. Which, to me, meant that I was pregnant. He said we wouldn't get married. He said that if I was pregnant, it was my problem, not his. I felt rejected. I brooded. Then I got angry with him. I told him if I was pregnant he should be a man, do the right thing by me and marry me. He laughed again and said I was stupid. He told me, "You can't get pregnant the first time." That eased my fear a bit, but I wasn't sure he was telling the truth. I was afraid he was wrong. I felt such shame and hurt and confusion that I began to cry. He hit me hard in the face. That was the only bruise I got on my face, from that last hit. I could feel it. I looked in the visor mirror and got another shock. I had never seen myself looking so disheveled and filthy before. I tried to clean up a bit and told him that now he'd really gotten me in trouble. My parents were going to know something had happened because of the way I looked. I cried more and he, gratefully, stopped responding to me.

He ended up not taking me home but dropping me off somewhere nearby. Literally "dropped" me off; he shoved me out of the car and threw my bicycle at me! He broke the front wheel rim on my bike so I couldn't ride it. I came walking down my street, lugging my broken bicycle, crying, and looking like hell. I knew my parents would be mad at me for being late and I was terrified that they would smack me around again. I never once thought of telling them what had happened. It wouldn't work as an excuse for my appearance and lateness. Plus, I had too much shame around the entire event. I couldn't imagine talking to them about something of that nature. We just didn't have that kind of relationship. I was for the most part a dutiful daughter who looked and acted properly and spoke when spoken to; they were the authority figures who ruled the roost. You did what they wanted, with little discussion.

Yet when I actually walked in the door, I had a strong, though fleeting, feeling of safety. Whatever else home meant to me, it was my home. My place to be in the big, scary world. When I walked in, I smelled familiar smells, felt familiar warmth, and recognized familiar "normalcy." These things were so pronounced after the extreme and difficult experience I'd just been through. Though frightened, I was very glad to be home. I wanted comfort and love.

My parents were waiting at the door. My mother had that special, disgusted anger in her voice when she said, "Where the hell have you been? Never mind, I don't want to know. Do you realize how late you are? What the hell were you thinking? Get out of my sight. You make me sick!" My father hit me, yelled something similar and with a look so damn disapproving and angry, said that he couldn't even look at me, either. They sent me to my room without dinner. I cried all night.

I got grounded for weeks. During those weeks I kept asking my parents, "Don't you even want to know what happened?" They kept saying they weren't interested. And even though no one, including me, had said a single word about that day's events, there was a new "protocol" in the house when dealing with me. My siblings also began avoiding me. If I hadn't felt horrible inside already, I certainly did then because of how they were all treating me. Eventually this led to a realization that my parents did know something had happened that day. Our relationship became even more strained with time and they looked at me less and less. My mom became more unpredictable in the way she spoke to me on a given day, and my dad just seemed angry and depressed.

What came after was more traumatic than the rape itself. I somehow could relate to Rob: He was just "screwed up." So was I. I instinctively knew that what made him treat me the way he did had everything to do with his own messed-up life. I even felt, at times, a kinship with him. But the rest of this horror story was beyond my comprehension, then and now. For at least two months I didn't tell a soul about the "thing" that had happened to me. I stopped getting my period. I "knew," without being told, that this was connected to what had happened that day. I didn't want to acknowledge it though, because I was trying to forget that day had ever happened. So, I tried to ignore my body's signals. I felt impending doom, but I just kept pushing it out of my mind and trying to go on "normally."

I ultimately could no longer fit into my school skirt (we wore uniforms at Catholic school). I decided to ask my friend, Patty, if she knew how you got pregnant. And what exactly being pregnant meant. (Was it something that you could make go away?) I told her I thought I might be, but I wouldn't tell her anything else. She knew "all about" sex and guys and everything else I was ignorant about. She asked me questions. Some I couldn't even answer. For one, I didn't know what "come" meant. She asked if I "did it." With my newfound knowledge of that term, I said yes. She asked if I had enjoyed it. I had blocked out so much of the event by then that I said no. I "knew" I shouldn't have. So I said I hadn't—even as I felt stirrings of shame regarding the physical sensations I had enjoyed. She told me that I had to enjoy it in order to get pregnant. That I had to be "wet"— or "come"—in order to get pregnant. I swore I hadn't done any of those things even though I wasn't sure what they all meant. I decided I couldn't possibly be pregnant. I went another few weeks in total confusion.

At some point, Patty started talking about when *she* was pregnant. (She was the type who always had to do you one better.) She said that she had had to have an abortion. I asked what that was. She told me that a doctor takes away the baby. I said, "What baby?" She said that being pregnant meant that you had a baby growing inside of you, which totally blew my mind! I suppose I had a little understanding of reproduction, somehow, but I'd refused to really believe it. In addition, I'd already discovered that even when I thought I knew something, I was usually wrong. My parents or other authorities would patiently explain to me that I "didn't have all the facts" or "I was too young to fully understand all that's involved".

Patty was now forcing me to listen to my inner suspicions, understand them, and accept them. I got really scared. She said that I could run away and have the baby. I considered that briefly and decided I couldn't do it, because my father would find me and kill me. Not figuratively, but literally. And even if no one found me, how would I live? I was just a kid! I'd only worked once, in my Dad's office, and didn't think I could earn a living. She constantly pressured me to tell her who I "did it" with. I couldn't tell her: I didn't want to remember any of it anymore and I was so deep down ashamed! Eventually we stopped being friends. She was my best friend—my only friend, really—up to that point, so it was devastating to lose her. My feeling of being alone in this horror hit deeper and deeper as time went on. I couldn't function in school. I couldn't think clearly. I started crying at the drop of a hat. It happened in class one day and the teacher sent me to the guidance office.

At the office I was sent to see Mr. McNeil. I was scared to go to him because I knew he'd tell my family! I felt so much shame that I couldn't say anything for at least an hour. I just sat in his office and cried. Finally, he said some things that made me decide that I had to trust someone. I started to tell him that I thought I was pregnant. He asked me if I had made love with anyone. I said no. He told me I must have if I was pregnant. I insisted I hadn't, so he asked me why I thought I was pregnant.

Now I felt I had to tell him the "other thing." I was so scared to speak of it, it took me another while to work up to it. When I finally started to relate the events of that day, he was totally sympathetic. He cried with me. He said he thought I was raped. I told him I didn't know what that word meant. I thought it just meant that someone beat you up and said mean things to you. He, again, was full of sympathy. He couldn't believe how little I knew. He wondered out loud why such an innocent little girl from such a good family should find herself in such a horrible predicament.

He explained what rape was, and then asked me if that described what had happened to me. I said yes, but I still didn't understand all the terms he used, such as "sexual abuse" and "sodomy." He ended up graphically explaining the terms, with tears coming down his face, and I lost all control. I realized, all of that had happened to me! I was mortified. He tried to explain that it wasn't my fault, but I didn't believe him. What he was talking about was so disgusting and dirty, and I had been a part of it! He tried to calm me down, but I was inconsolable. I knew my father and mother would never accept all of this. I knew my brother and sister would be ashamed of me. The whole world would be, I felt. I briefly thought of killing myself.

Mr. McNeil explained that we had the more urgent problem of the pregnancy to deal with first. After that, he said that I would be best helped by the school psychiatrist. I asked him what a psychiatrist was. He explained and set up an appointment for me to see Dr. Cleary. Then he dropped the bomb: he said we had to tell my parents.

As I heard the words, adrenaline coursed through me. My heart thumped fast and loud in my chest, and I got dizzy and weak. The fear reached a high point, then drained as though a plug had been pulled. I must have briefly passed out. When I came to, I cried for another half hour. I was so scared that I was shaking from head to foot. I explained that my father wouldn't understand. That he would hurt me. Mr. McNeil knew my parents through my brother Stan, The Wonderman. He was a scholar, a gentleman, an excellent athlete and everything parents could want in a son, and everything a sister could want in a brother, too. I loved him dearly, and I was proud of him. This, somehow, compounded my shame. Having come in contact with my parents through Stan, (of course) Mr. McNeil thought they were wonderful. But he didn't know what went on at home. And I wouldn't, couldn't, tell him, either. It was too shameful. I couldn't ruin my father's reputation like that. In fact, my parents had instructed us kids many times to never tell another living soul what went on behind our closed doors.

So, I didn't go into detail about why I couldn't tell my mother and father, but I insisted that we not. He calmed me down and asked me what I thought my options were if I didn't appeal to my parents for help. As I thought about it, I remembered my conversation with my friend, Patty, and blurted out that I could run away. He looked very sad and said that, yes, there were halfway houses that I could live in until the baby was born, but what about the rest of my life? Wouldn't it be better if I included my parents in this? I said no. Then I remembered Patty's abortion. So I asked about that. He was against abortion and told me that it was not an option. He said it was against my faith. My faith? What the hell did he know about my faith? I told him that my God would not want me to have to live with what my parents would do to me if we told them everything. My God would rather I have an abortion. That pretty much ended the discussion. Mr. McNeil, for all his good-heartedness, was not open minded about this issue. He told me I was being sacrilegious and that talking about God that way was blasphemous (He had once been a priest). I think I lost any last vestige of faith in the Catholic Church on that day.

Mr. McNeil asked me which parent I wanted to call first. I chose my father. Dad, at least, was stable most of the time. Mom could fly off the handle at burnt toast! But Dad was usually as calm as possible—until, of course, he blew. But that wasn't often (though when it did happen, he would hit me very hard). Although at that point I figured I was "dead meat," I thought Mr. McNeil could partially protect me—that my Dad would get caught if he killed me or sent me away. I was pretty sure Mr. McNeil would ask questions if he never saw me again. So Mr. McNeil called my Dad. I was immobile with fear, and didn't hear the phone conversation at all.

After a seemingly endless wait, my father arrived and a new discomfort began. I'd never been in a situation where an outside adult had the goods on me and was about to explain it to one of my parents—with me sitting right there! I was twisted up inside and squeezing my hands in fists so hard that my knuckles were white and my nails were digging holes in my hands. I didn't say a word for the first twenty minutes or so; Mr. McNeil did all the talking. I just sat there feeling ashamed of myself and dreading what would happen to me.

My father surprised me. He seemed very upset, but upset for me, not at me. There was a caring look in his eyes, and tears, as he looked at me while Mr. McNeil spoke. Oh, I wanted so badly to be held by my Daddy at that moment! I wanted him to make everything better again. Make this inner pain go away and tell me he loved me, and that he was sorry I had had to go through such a painful experience. When the explanation was over, my Dad thanked Mr. McNeil and mentioned that he and my Mom would have to talk about this. He said that everything would be okay and he stood up to leave. Mr. McNeil looked at me and said, "See? I knew your Dad would help you. He loves you, Mary. You're his daughter. You're going to be alright." I smiled and hugged my Dad and we walked out of the office, toward the front entrance of the school. I was feeling so much better that I decided I'd try to finish out the school day.

As I was walking away my Dad said, "Mary, we'll talk when you get home." I thought I heard sternness in his voice, but I dismissed it because of the caring interaction I had just had with him in Mr. McNeil's office. I turned back to him and smiled (a shame-faced smile, with a little trepidation beginning to rise) and went to hug him again. I was about to say thank you but I noticed he wasn't returning my hug. My blood was already draining again when my Dad very quietly said, "Don't think this makes everything okay, Mary. You did the worst possible thing you could ever do in your life, and I'm disgusted with you. You're an embarrassment to me and your mother. How could you go to that man? Do you want to ruin your brother, too? What the hell is wrong with you, anyway? Your brother has to go to school here, you know. Maybe we'll take you out of this school and put you in public school. I hope this doesn't reflect badly on Stan. I'm sick! You make me sick! I don't know what your mother will do, but you'd better pray she doesn't disown you like she did your sister. I don't know if I can stand to see you after this, either." And with that, he left.

Immediately, the bottom dropped out. The foyer walls disappeared and everything turned gray. I went through the front door to the outside and noticed that it, too, was gray. But that's the extent of what I saw. I smoked a cigarette and walked aimlessly. I had nowhere to go. I was completely alone in the world with this incredible weight on my shoulders. I thought, "I can't live with this. I just can't." Then I crumpled to the ground and cried. Eventually I became aware that I was a spectacle in the middle of the school grounds and figured I should get up and find a way home. I don't remember how I got home. Nothing seemed real anymore; nothing mattered. I'd gone inside somewhere. I don't remember much of the daily incidentals for a while after that.

I have a sketchy memory of seeing my mother for the first time after my Dad found out. It was briefly painful, then I shut down. My mother told me she knew I'd "wanted it," that I wasn't raped, that I had "asked for it." She called me a whore and slut and told me I was just like my sister (had this happened to my sister, I wondered?) and that she couldn't stand the sight of me. She kept telling me I'd jeopardized my father's reputation. I couldn't grasp what she meant. She said I'd ruined my brother, as well (what brother? I couldn't remember him at the moment). Where I'd go to school after this was in question. I didn't care. I barely listened. I was already dead, as far as I could tell. None of what she said mattered. She hit me and spit and screamed and ranted and I saw it all as if watching a movie. Sometimes I couldn't remember who she was. Sometimes I couldn't remember what she was talking about. Who is this woman yelling at? What is she saying? What happened? A big man got into the scene. Oh, my father, that's right. He's hitting, too. It doesn't hurt. Did he just hit me? I can't feel it. I'm so tired. I want to go to sleep and never wake up.

Some part of me must have been paying better attention because I internalized all that was said. I believed every last nasty comment made about me. I began to shift, somewhere inside, to their side. I began to hate me, too. How could I do this to them? How could a person be so stupid? I deserve everything that happens for being so ignorant. I must have wanted that guy to do what he did. They must be right. What a vile human being I am. I don't deserve to live. I should die. God! I wanted to die!

Another shift occurred. I found myself crying and praying constantly. "God, help me understand. Why me? Why is all of this happening?" I was in hell, and I couldn't find a way out. Soon after this shift, I was scheduled to see Dr. Cleary. I told my parents (wanting to be accepted again, get things back to normal) the morning of the appointment. They made me cancel while they stood by at the phone and watched. They told me I could just "get over it" because they weren't paying for me to tell the world about our family and talk badly about them. Because they knew I'd blame everything on them.

I was completely devastated that they wouldn't let me talk to anyone. It must have been the final straw. I didn't realize that I had wanted so badly to talk to someone who, in Mr. McNeil's words, "helps people understand themselves and put the pieces of their lives back together after tragedy." He was an expert at helping people like me and I so needed help. But my parents took it away. My last hope was gone and I'd sunk as low as one could go. Or so I thought.

One night sometime later, my father told me I was not going to school the next day but I had to get up early. I was through asking questions, so I just listened and acted accordingly. I woke up and got dressed in corduroys. They were too tight and I was embarrassed, but they were the only casual clothes I had. My parents and I got in the car and began the mysterious trip in silence. After thirty minutes of letting my mind wander dangerously I finally asked where we were going. My mother turned around immediately and began verbally abusing me. My father chimed in here and there in agreement. I clammed up. I was then told several times to "wipe that puss off your face!"

After a long period of silence, my mother asked me if I knew what "we" were doing. I said no, because of course I didn't. In a martyr-like tone she informed me that she and my father were "taking care of the biggest mistake I had ever made in my life." And that I better not ever forget it. I owed them my life, she said (an old tune). I shut down again. I figured I was going off to die. I accepted it. Even welcomed it, actually. I was already dead inside anyway. What was there to live for? So I sat quietly, waiting to get "there." Wherever "there" was. It took a long time. I figured we were going far away from our community so that no one would ever know what really had happened. I'd just disappear.

Finally we were at a hospital. My parents were talking to each other as if I weren't there, deciding which way to go, wondering if they had everything they needed, if they should get food, and so on. I just followed along silently. We were in a lobby of sorts when my mother's attitude changed and she expressed sympathy for what I was about to go through. I didn't know what was going to happen so it didn't mean much. I didn't ask because I was tired of being so stupid and having to ask questions. I figured it didn't matter anymore anyway. My father, upon seeing my mother behaving so sympathetically, said to me, "You know, this is killing your mother. She hates that her little girl has to go through this. I hope you appreciate that!" I remained numb.

We got to the proper floor and my mother bailed out. She couldn't go to the nurse's desk with me. My father took me. That was when I started to get scared. I began asking rapid-fire questions in a shrill voice. My father told me the nurses would explain everything. I asked where my mother was. He said she had gone to the cafeteria. I was bereft. I wanted my Mommy, suddenly. I really thought they were leaving me behind to be killed by some doctor, as they had done with our family dog. I knew nothing of laws; all I knew was that whatever my parents wanted in life, they got. If they wanted me dead but couldn't do it themselves, I thoroughly believed they could find someone to do it for them. I was never more afraid in my life than at that moment. I was also never more humbled or ashamed or sorry for existing. I had to pee. I had to scream. I had to get out of there!

No, I had to stay, I was told. I was being forced to go along with my death. Then I began to think that maybe this was a mental ward. My parents weren't going to have me killed; they would just put me away here, for the rest of my life. I gave in at that point. I followed directions obediently and thought my life, as I knew it, was over. I didn't matter anyway. Maybe this was better.

I was led to a room where there were about five women completely covered up in beds. They were asleep. I thought that made sense. There was no light in the room. There was nothing to do but sleep. This is how I would live. Just like them.

Then I was given a hospital gown to wear. My mother walked into the room, and handed me my own pajamas and a bathrobe and slippers. The nurse said I couldn't wear them. I cried and my mother went to bat for me. The nurse yelled, "the reason she can't wear them, Mrs. Grant, is because they'll get all bloody." I could put them on after the "procedure." My mother seemed to understand and told me to listen to the nurses. She kissed me once and said she'd be back that night. I felt a glimmer of hope and obeyed the nurse. But I didn't know what the "procedure" was. I remembered a movie about a guy who had a part of his brain removed because there was something wrong with the way he behaved. I thought, maybe, they were going to do that to me. Maybe it would help me, I reasoned. But I was afraid it would hurt.

I noticed a crossword puzzle book on my bed that my mother must have left. I was very grateful. She knew I liked to do crosswords. So did she. In fact, it was the one fun thing we ever did together. Seeing the book made me feel close to my Mom, somehow. I thought it meant she really did care about me. So I just stayed in bed and did crossword puzzles and tried not to think.

A few hours later the same nurse came back in with a few new girls. Some were real big in the stomach, and I began to think that I might be there for something to do with my stomach! This must be what Patty meant by abortion! Hurray! I wasn't going to die and I wouldn't be pregnant anymore! All hope returned after this realization, and I went along with everything I was told. I wanted to help them any way I could!

The nurse told us to "all gather around for a talk." She described what would "probably happen" to all of us. Unless, she said, we were "farther along." Then, she said, the "procedure" would be a little different, but didn't describe how. She then gave us some instructions and left the room. Another person I'd never seen before now came in and put a needle into my arm and told me I would have to go to the bathroom a lot. Boy was she ever right! All of "us girls" started laughing about how often we were going to the bathroom, and the bother of having to drag a bottle on a hook on wheels in with us. But I noticed some girls didn't have a needle and a bottle attached to them.

The nurses kept coming into the room and taking one girl at a time from the room. After a while I became worried because all the girls who had left had come back, slept, and had already left. Why hadn't I left the room yet? And some of those girls' boyfriends, mothers, fathers, and husbands had come, but not my Mom. Why?

Finally it was my turn. They wheeled me into a very small room with a lot of people in it. A nice nurse talked to me while she got me over to a corner of the room. She said the doctor was going to examine me now. The doctor turned around just then with a clear glove on his hand and said, "scoot down!" I wasn't sure what he meant and the nurse helped me get my butt to the end of the table. When I was where I needed to be, he said, "Put your feet in the stirrups!" Stirrups? That was a horse term! I looked at the end of the table and saw what looked like stirrups attached to it. He must mean those, I thought. I put my feet in them and felt very exposed. I closed my knees. I was very scared. The only other time someone had stood in that spot looking to get near that part of me…I didn't even want to think about that.

The doctor said, "Open your legs. We haven't got all day, here." He tried to pry my legs open but I wasn't cooperating. He looked angry and said, "C'mon, honey! It's not like you haven't done this before!" I was ashamed and hurt and angry. In an attempt to explain my uncooperative state, I said, "I was raped, you know!" He replied, "Yeah. I know. Everyone says that. It's amazing how many women I see say they were raped. C'mon, spread em!" I did and he stuck his finger in me! I was feeling just like I had when Rob had rammed his penis in me. I was very, very scared. The nurse said it was okay, and told me not to pay attention to the doctor. She stroked my hair and said to hang on, it was almost over. The doctor said I was "too far along" and called to some guy. They started talking about me, and the nurse looked at me, worriedly. Then she wheeled me over to another man who was really nice.

This new man got close to my head and started talking softly. He said that he would never do what he was about to if he didn't have to. He had to, though. He said it was important that I stay still and not move. That if I moved I could get badly hurt or cut or something. He asked me if I was strong. He asked me about my "pain tolerance." I said something to the effect that I was strong and could handle pain. He said that was good because I needed to be. He then showed me these really long needles. I nearly passed out at the sight of them! He said he had to put these really long needles into my belly, just below my belly button, and take the fluid out of the sac. Then he had to replace the fluid with another kind that would kill the fetus. I didn't understand it all but I knew it would hurt. I cried a little and he comforted me. Then he swabbed an iodine solution over my belly and I gasped and jerked! I immediately apologized, worried I'd ruined everything. He said it was his fault. He'd forgotten to tell me he was going to do that. Now he was going to do the needle thing, so hang on!

He did it. It hurt, but not too bad. I just couldn't look. When it was all over he said he was proud of me. So was I. I was strong. Then they wheeled me out and back to my room.

Either that night or the next, I started to feel like I had to go to the bathroom, and I was doubled over in pain. I couldn't believe how bad I hurt! A very nice nurse heard me and came in to the room. She gave me a bedpan and told me not to try to get up for the bathroom. Just to do it in the bedpan. I said I couldn't! I was bladder-shy. She said it wouldn't be coming from my bladder. She said to push as if I was going "number two." I did, over and over. Nothing happened. She got called away and then it happened! I felt a huge gush. Relief came over me and then pain again.

I thought my insides had fallen out! I screamed. The nurse came running back and shushed me. She said I would scare the other girls who hadn't been through it yet. Then she had to leave again. I looked in the bedpan and saw a little baby. It almost looked fake—it was tiny, half the size of my hand! There was so much blood and it was scary to look at. The nurse came running back and said, "Shit! I'm so sorry, honey! You weren't supposed to see that! I was just so busy I couldn't be here long enough!" I consoled her, and told her it wasn't that bad. It was reality, and I had to face it. She said I was a good girl. Then she cleaned me up.

Then she flushed the bedpan contents down the toilet. I couldn't believe it! She said that's what they did. Then she told me to be prepared because there was more. I couldn't believe that, either. She said I probably would feel more pain soon and then another gush would come. Sure enough, that's what happened. Boy, did it hurt! After all the gushing, I started to get strong cramping. She explained what was happening and gave me a pill to contract my uterus. Eventually, I fell asleep.

At last, they told me to get dressed. My parents would be there soon. I didn't want to see them and I wanted to run into their arms all at the same time. My dad was the only one to show up. I no longer had a "mommy," I had a "mother." I even called her that for a few months after. She hated it. I was glad.

We never talked about it. Ever. The only reference my parents made to it was about how much money it had cost. Every now and then, my mother would tell me they were still paying for it. She'd tell me that I owed them. I would say, "I was raped! I don't owe you anything! I never said I even wanted an abortion!" She'd usually smack me, and say, "Bullshit! You were 'raped'—please! How convenient for you!" I hated them both for years. And, of course, did everything I could to make it up to them, too. Outwardly I'd be adamant in my defense regarding the rape. Inwardly, however, I felt like the lowest form of scum on earth. As they told me I was, over and over, for years.

*Editor's Note: The author has used a pseudonym for the purpose of this anthology.

MY ADULT LIFE IN SIX EASY INSTALLMENTS

Kathleen George Kearney

1. Conception: The Prologue

I am sitting with the lover on a bed.

We would have cigarettes on our lips, if either of us smoked.

We are late, the both of us. Usually, we take turns being the first to leave. We never go together; that would mean something to the neighbors next door, and we prefer to remain *mysterious* (in our words) and *casual* (in theirs). In the morning routine, someone is the first to leave, breaking the luminous moment with wrinkled clothes and the wrong shirt. It is customary to lean in on the bed to kiss good-bye. Such a kiss is long enough to say something about the night before (*I'm sorry, Thanks for listening, Yes you are beautiful in the morning*), yet short enough to commit to nothing about the day ahead. Then the one who is dressed will leave, will try on the sunlight of the day and mosey off to the professional world. Whoever is left in the bed will daydream for a while before cleaning up, erasing the traces of the night: sheets are straightened, or changed, or covered up with blankets. Cats are soothed. Beer bottles are recycled. Calls from friends are returned.

But today, we stay on the bed. No one is dressed. No one has read the paper in order to know what to be angry about today. And the cats are hiding. He has called the store, telling them that he will be there soon, ready to sell expensive greeting cards made of rough paper where the plant leaves and flower stalks are still visible. Among those cards, and the Magnetic Poetry and the coeds who still love to collect stickers, he will dream of the novels he will write.

"We've always been so careful," he says with disbelief.

I murmur agreement, following the route of a crack in the ceiling plaster.

"I don't think it's going to happen," he says with confidence. A pause. " But what would we do if it did?"

We talk about decisions as if they are candy. When you don't have the candy, you are so sure that you know what it tastes like; you have political stances which rest entirely on the truth of this confection. But then, the day comes when you receive the candy, and it is in fact not what you thought it was at all. That night you have it in your mouth as you dream and when morning comes you brush your teeth over and over and over again. But you still feel the sugar, rough and smothering. And you realize that you are going to live a long time.

"I can't imagine it happening to a woman like you," he says as he folds his body over a new sheet, and brushes out my hair with his fingers.

I am not sure whether I should be insulted or relieved.

He stretches for a moment, watching his own muscles as if they are new. The lover wishes he could dance. His hair is longer than mine. He strides out the door and down the hall. He is singing in a haze of light becoming bitter: "Call me if anything happens."

2. Embryo: The Decision

I am sitting in a phone booth with the younger brother on the other end of the line.

The coffee shop is full of people like me: folks with props of books and newspapers and letters to write, who are here to be distracted, not productive.

"So, are you all right?" he asks.

I say all of the usual things, what I have heard many friends say before me: *I am as good as I can be. Nauseated all the time. Tired. Feeling like a freak, like everyone who looks at me can tell, like I am the only smart woman who has messed up like this.*

"When did you find out?" The brother shuffles the receiver. I can hear the toddler babbling in the background.

I remember holding the wet blue cross in my hand last night. It came straight out of one of those commercials where the couple holding the blue cross are happy, happy, happy, and you loathe them and swear that you will never act like that when it's your turn. A wet blue cross. Strange symbol for the cause at hand. Isn't blue the color of wisdom?

"Are you going to get married?"

He is naïve, the younger brother. He married a girlfriend right after high school graduation, and the baby came five months later. The younger brother works second shift, watches the son in the mornings, and tries to take a course or two at the community college on weekends.

He has heard my tirade about marriage, because I gave it to him the night before the wedding. We stood in a humid evening outside of a potluck supper held at the Elk's Club, and were buzzed on that very particular taste of beer from tin cans. I was naïve to think I could be influential at that point.

No way. I'm not going through with it.

Silence on his end. The son is banging on what are no doubt pots and pans used as a dwarf drum set.

A man waits outside the phone booth, trying not to let me know that he is anxious. I chose a coffee shop for confession because it is one of the few places where one can have a private stage in the midst of a public working on its own theatrics. The patrons pass each other in a maze of mismatched tables and chairs, bodies just close enough to declare that they are strangers to one another.

"It's sad. But I'll go with you, if you want. I can come up this weekend."

A nice offer, but he'll miss his Introduction to Philosophy class.

"Okay, then. Call me when it's over."

3. Fetus: First Conversation

I am sitting with the older brother at dinner.

He pretends that he isn't shocked, that he knew this is what we would come to all along: a strained conversation where we lean over that bright scarlet divide, where he can say:

"I'm here for you, no matter what you decide."

The older brother has what is called a "good" position at an environmental consulting firm. This enables him to be smug and sincere, with all four ESPN channels and the gall to vote against school levies. We have never been compatriots before. In years past, we perfected two battling jungles: *Fascist, and Feminazi*. Now he wants to assume there's a truce. Now he drums a rhythm with his fingers on the tablecloth. Four years at an almost-Ivy League school did not prepare him for this.

A server brings him another Rob Roy. The older brother wouldn't let me have one.

He sips his drink. He drinks Rob Roys because that is what the father drinks. The father is far away, in the small, smoldering town where the older brother, the younger brother and I were raised. He is also known as the Major, because he brought Vietnam home with him.

I watch another family across the room, kissing and hugging for one another in a show of unity so sincere that they must practice it only once or twice a year, perhaps an anniversary.

Family is just a trip somebody took, and the only thing brought home is a cheap plastic snow globe, bought in a rut on the interstate, with flakes of white arching over an idealized landscape where the sky reads *The Weather is Here, Wish You Were Fine*.

So it is over asparagus in peppered butter and pear tart with raspberry crème sauce ("Order whatever you want; you need your strength," he told me in the car) that the older brother tries to reach me, to soothe the drama with: "Don't worry, I have a friend who works at a clinic," and "I wouldn't tell Mom and Dad if I were you," and "Shouldn't you call and tell *him*?"

4. Induced: Bleeding

I am sitting on a bed again, this time with the roommate.

He hovers over me like a renegade midwife. He has been perfecting an intricate persecution complex for years, and now he revels so much in the chance to be the savior that he almost thanks me. He shuts the curtains (always dusty) and screens the in-coming phone calls. He shoves at me cups of hot sassafras tea in cracked mugs, a different mug each time, with Impressionistic reproductions on each one. Our neighborhood homeopath has informed me of exactly which herbs will increase the contractions, and which will relieve the cramping. He worries that I will lose too much blood, but not enough of the tissue.

He told me not to do it this way.

He told me to swallow my private pride and think of it as a chance for solidarity.

He canceled a date with his boyfriend to stay with me.

The phone rings, the answering machine picks up, and someone's mother is sharing news of the hometown and wondering why *Dear* hasn't called. I have no idea whose mother it is. Mopping up my fever, he doesn't seem to care.

He has offered to massage my abdomen. That's how the birthing women do it in Indonesia. I am told he learns these things on cable T.V. He calls a doctor in hushed tones, as if I don't already know what is happening to me.

"How long?" he is repeating into the phone. "Oh, God, all night. I suppose, five or six hours…No, she's not that far along…Yes, I have checked the linens and the toilet, but she told me not to save anything…I agree. Yes, I'll bring her in right now."

The roommate tells me we are leaving, whether I like it or not. He takes away cloth and sweat and tears and blood, and he is not made sick, as so many men are. I will love him forever for that.

He stares deep into my belly, and asks, "Should we say a prayer?"

I set my head back in the pool of the sheets. I have already said my prayers. Now I am nearly drowning in them.

Shrugging into the washcloth as if to find some meaning in its patterns, he says: "I guess there's no need to call *him* now."

5. Dilation & Curettage: Liberation

I am sitting on an exam table with the resident hanging over me.

This is the first time he has done this. He shifts his weight from hip to hip, swinging back and forth. His arms are crossed in front of his chest. Perhaps he is trying to look worried for me, about me, but it is clear he is thinking of himself. Afterward, he can write this one down in his journal, call his friends from medical school to see if they have encountered this yet.

The emergency room clangs and shouts and wheels around us.

I dare him to ask me what I did, what I took, what in the hell I was thinking. But he will not ask. He doesn't want to know the answers.

He clears his throat: "There is tissue retained in your uterus. We have to remove it. And we have to stop the bleeding. You could hemorrhage. This procedure is very simple, although you will experience some cramping—"

I hold up my hand. *Yes, Yes, D&C, open & scrape*, I know the lingo. I served my time in the underground women's health movement during college. Those early nineties.

"We can give you anesthesia if you like."

I refuse, pull the blanket tighter around me. He has told me that with an hour more at home, I would have gone into shock. I imagine that shock is a religious experience.

"All right, then, we'll move forward with the procedure. Have you been through this before?"

No, never, and yes, all the time—with sisters, with friends, with the loves of old friends, in all my previous girlhoods. I feel as if I already wrote this night. I put it in a poem that the first-year writing professor called *almost* profound. Fate is a trickster. Destiny is a puzzle, not a page in the schedule. This was never meant to be. This was always meant to be.

I am still feverish.

He fiddles with the cloth tie sewn into the waistband of his scrubs. They are deep blue. Very hip. "I'll go tell your husband."

I shake my head. *He's not my husband. He's not even on my team.*

He is embarrassed. Trying to be sensitive, but falling on his face. No doubt the med school cronies will have something to say about that. "I'm sorry. Not because he isn't your husband, but...Well, you know. I'm just...sorry."

Just sorry? I think about what I feel. *Just liberation. Relief. A strange calm despite not knowing whether the life I have made is beginning or ending.*

He looks at me with an amazement that tells me this is a story he can't find in the anecdotal research. This is not a fable he can make his buddies understand.

He wants more information. But I am not disclosing. I swing my legs up on the table. *Let's get it over with, then.*

"Oh," he says again. "Then you can go ahead and cancel your appointment, if you made one." He walks through the line of curtains. Then he turns back: "Walking through those protesters is a bitch, anyway."

6. Post-D&C: Postscript

I am sitting with a friend at a bar.

He is protective and worried: "Are you sure you should be drinking?"

I raise my bottle as if to toast some invisible wish. I am saluting my resurrection. But I don't know if he has ever been in the waiting room—any waiting room, or walked by screaming pickets, or wondered when the life he made began. I don't want to get into it with him. I shrug, *it's all over but the shouting.* Only nobody shouts afterwards.

He looks down at the wine stains on the floor, flowing against the grain of the wood, where the truth may be carved by some sad or wistful woman who came before me.

"I keep thinking of a scene I remember from Sunday school." The friend is a student in the seminary, and he always speaks as if we are in church. Many nights, the bar is a church for him, a sanctuary where whatever judgments he makes about lovers and brothers and witnesses along the way is written as gospel and then burned at the end of the evening by the moon following him as he walks home. The friend likes to speak in riddles. Just like Jesus.

"It's the scene that people always like to paint, the one where the angel announces to Mary that she will bear Christ." It doesn't matter to the friend that I have not been in church for years. "And in so many of the old paintings, it's as if the sun exploded in that moment, and Mary is in the center of the explosion, and even the angel is blinded…"

I nod into my ale. I know this one.

He stares off at an angry, mute television, and at himself beyond it in a mirror. "I imagine that the bursting wasn't really about having this messiah called Jesus. I like to imagine that the explosion was actually very simple. It wasn't about theology. The explosion was just her life running through her. It didn't matter what she said or did or thought. In the end, there was only Mary, swimming in her own life."

He offers me no tea in which to sob, no bed in which to rest, no marriage into which to run, no candy to get stuck in, no salvific dinner plate. "Was that what it was like?…Was it?"

The moments of my life flood out from the blue water of his eyes meeting mine.

I take my pause in this scene, because I have been waiting for it.

The beer reflects nothing.

Sure, it was like that. I can only hope it was like that.

A CHOICE BETWEEN TERRIBLE AND AWFUL

Nicole Foster[*]

I spent the first twenty-eight years of my life in the silent majority of pro-choice Americans, confident that my rights were protected, never knowing that this issue would affect me in such a personal way.

From the beginning, he was not what I expected. We weren't planning to have our second child at that time. When I saw those two lines on the home pregnancy test, I started to cry, and they weren't tears of joy. We were barely scraping by on two incomes and having trouble adjusting to parenthood. Our daughter was just over eighteen months old, and I felt positively overwhelmed. By the time I went to my first prenatal appointment, I had adjusted to the idea enough to be horrified when my doctor asked me if we planned to continue the pregnancy. Then she spun her magic wheel and announced, "The due date will be, well, let's see here, December 25th." She looked hesitantly at me as a big grin spread over my face. "A Christmas baby," I thought, "How cool!" I didn't pay much attention as she discussed the pregnancy routine. After all, I'd done this before. I knew what to expect.

The pregnancy proceeded along normally; we were excited for our first sonogram at nineteen weeks. We had a daughter and were hoping for a son. The sonogram would reveal the sex. It lasted a little longer than we expected; the technician called in a doctor to review the image. They told us we were having a boy and sent us home with our videotape. I thought it was a little weird when the doctor said, "Your doctor will call you," but I quickly suppressed any inkling of fear I felt, and sat down at home to watch the tape. My husband returned to work to show off the sonogram pictures they had given us. About three hours later, my obstetrician called and said, "I have some bad news. Wait, I'm sorry, I'll have to call you back." I stood there holding the phone, frozen, in complete disbelief. This could not be happening.

After the longest fifteen minutes of my life, she called back with the news that our baby had Spina Bifida. I asked her what that meant for the pregnancy. She said that they wanted me to come back to her office so they could get a "better look." Feeling numb, I hung up the phone. It was a Friday afternoon, and we had no idea where to turn for help or information. We spent the weekend in a daze, looking for information, and finding very little. At that time, we were a world away from the cyber-realm, which today provides us with instant access to all kinds of medical information. On Monday, the technician confirmed that our baby had Spina Bifida, and showed us where the lesion was located on his spine. Our doctor admitted that if she were in this situation, she would terminate the pregnancy. In the back of my mind, I wondered if termination was something that we should consider. But, we spent the next week talking to a variety of specialists: a pediatric neurosurgeon, two neo-natal Intensive Care Unit (ICU) doctors, a lady from the Spina Bifida Association, and a nurse who ran the Spina Bifida clinic at our local hospital. It was through one of them that we got a referral to a specialist in ultrasonography. We felt that we needed more information on this baby's prognosis, and hoped this specialist could give it to us.

Often we look back on these horrendous times and see little glimpses of the positive. This specialist was one of those glimpses. He and his staff were full of support, sympathy and, yes, even hugs. After a very thorough look, the doctor told us that he believed our baby's defect would not be that severe. He felt that there was a good chance that the defect might be closed, which meant a lot less neurological damage. He specifically mentioned that the hydrocephalus, a condition common in babies with neural tube defects, where excess fluid builds up in the brain, was "so mild that you wouldn't even know it was there if we hadn't measured for it."

After a week of agony, we had hope. He recommended a new obstetrician for us. We were ecstatic. I couldn't wait to go back to my old obstetrician with my baby son, and show her how wrong her initial prognosis had been. I strongly felt that we would be beat the odds!

After four weeks went by, my new doctor scheduled another sonogram to see how things were going. We watched our son move, enjoying every moment. Afterwards, I returned to work, and showed off all of the pictures. When the doctor called me later that day, I was totally unprepared for what he said. "The hydrocephalus has gotten significantly worse." He explained that in cases like this one, the odds were that my son would be stillborn or die shortly after birth. You would think that I would've been bracing myself for this possibility, but instead, it was like getting hit by a Mack truck. That night, our obstetrician called to say, "I know you're not going to like this, but I think we should wait one more week and then check again." I didn't like it, but in a way, it put off the monumental decision that I knew was coming. I proceeded along as if everything was going to be fine. I even bought a hat for my son that weekend. After the next sonogram, my doctor was in tears as he told us that our son's condition hadn't changed. We were scheduled to meet with the obstetrician later that morning to discuss the options. I screamed at my husband, "I will not consider ending this pregnancy unless they tell us there is no hope." A few hours later, sitting in our obstetrician's office, he told us there was no hope.

As I absorbed this horrible news, I had no idea that more was coming: I could not get an abortion this late in the pregnancy anywhere in Texas. (By that time I was twenty-six weeks into my pregnancy.) "Here is the name of a doctor in Wichita, Kansas." The obstetrician explained that he had talked to the office staff at the clinic, and they seemed really nice. We left in silence. I was barely able to stand up as I rode down the elevator to my car. "How can this be happening," I screamed inside my head. When we got home, I sat down to make the call to Kansas, while my husband listened in on the other line. I will never forget the voice on the other end of the line. It was comforting, competent, and supportive. She had answers to all of my questions and tried to prepare me for the week ahead. At the end of our conversation she said, "I don't know if you're aware of this, but the doctor is the one who was shot last week." How many times could I ask, "How much worse can this get," only to find out that the answer was, "It can get a hell of a lot worse." All of a sudden, I felt a new emotion: fear. Fear for my safety and for the safety of the only person in the United States who was willing to help us. Now a news report about a doctor being shot, which had previously seemed a world away, was way too close to home.

We waited four long days to make the trip to Kansas. After we checked into our hotel, we drove to the clinic to check it out. Seeing it at night, closed and quiet, would not prepare us for what was ahead the next morning. As we drove up to the clinic, there were crowds of protesters, yelling, holding signs, and trying to block our car. I was shaking as I walked into the clinic and had to go through a metal detector and present identification to the staff. "Don't worry," they told us, "you won't have to do this every day." Oh joy. We were ushered into a special room where there were three other families. Three other families who had come from all over the country, to do something that was breaking their hearts.

How could this happen? Why didn't I know that it could be this difficult to make a personal choice, a choice that we believed was preventing a lifetime of suffering for our son? The doctor still had scabs from the shooting, but he walked into the room smiling and, by some miracle, had all of us smiling by the time the talk was over. That night, he again met with all of us to talk about our losses and the grief that was accompanying them. He urged us to take the grief process seriously and offered any service that would make it easier for us. If we desired, he said we would be able to hold our babies, baptize our babies, and have photos of our babies. He warned us that if we tried to suppress the grief, it would find its way out somehow. It felt so good to finally talk to others who were going through this, and to a doctor who supported us and understood how truly heartbreaking this situation was for us.

Over the next four days, I went through the labor and delivery process. My son was stillborn on September 16, 1993 and, a few hours later, I was able to see him, to hold him, and to say good bye. I will never be able to express how grateful I am to the doctor at the clinic for his compassionate care, especially in the face of such very real personal risk. Not a day goes by that I don't miss my son. But there are some other left-over emotions. The main one is anger.

First, I am angry with the vocal minority who spew their hateful, anti-abortion rhetoric all over the place. They do not know me. They did not love my son. Yet they judge me, and they judge every woman who walks through those clinic doors. Why are they so bold and fearless in espousing their views, while those of us who have strong beliefs to the contrary are afraid to speak up? Why are we afraid to speak up? What is it in the foundation of my psyche that causes me to feel tormented by guilt for wanting to spare my son a short, pain-filled life? Why is abortion the "scarlet A?"

Second, I am angry at organized religion. Although there are many denominations that will speak out against abortion rights, there are also many that support abortion rights. As far as I'm concerned, they are not doing nearly enough to educate everyone about the fact that there is, and always has been, strong religious support for choice. There are many churches that boldly place white crosses on their lawns in memory of "murdered" babies. Where are the churches displaying crosses in memory of women killed by botched, illegal abortions, or the thousands of walking wounded who have lost their spiritual homes because they feel tainted by this experience? Why are there no support groups? And if there were support groups, would anyone have the courage to show her face at one?

Finally, I am angry with myself for being completely oblivious to the state of abortion rights in this country. I am embarrassed to admit that I never thought that this issue would affect me, and because of that, I never took the time to really learn what was going on in the abortion arena. It has been over five years since I went through this life-altering experience. I am one of the "lucky" ones. I was able to go on to have two more healthy sons. I have been able to "move on." At least that is what people tell me. They are so relieved when they say, "Well, it seems like you're really doing well." And yes, five years later, I still want to scream at them, "I am not doing well, I feel tormented!"

Growing up, there was no shortage of anti-choice rhetoric. Even today, I can hardly ever read a Letters to the Editor section without encountering an anti-choice letter full of misinformation. And I wonder, "Where is the outcry? Where are the masses of us who have experienced this? Why does no one write in to refute these lies? Why does my fear and guilt keep me from speaking out? How much erroneous information will I listen to? How many more people will be killed? How much more will our rights erode before I overcome my guilt and fear and speak out?" Or, maybe the better question is, will I ever overcome my guilt and fear, and speak out about my experience? And if the answer is no, how can I live with that?

*Editor's Note: The author has used a pseudonym to protect her privacy.

MY STORY

Suzanne Seas*

We talk at dinner, asking questions,
making agreements on what we'll use
when we have sex.

At 3 am he presses against me.
In the dark of passion the plan is forgotten,
the rush of pleasure thoughtless
the crisis
Inconceivable.

He sleeps huddled at my side, his breath deep and slow.
I lie awake in terror, tears on my face.
Somehow I know, without question.
I have a child.

Six hours later, I take pills in a white sterile office.
Kill it before it grows.
Oh God, please kill it.
I know it's there.

I drive on a forty below winter day
To his cabin in the woods
and lie on the floor waiting for him.
I am sick.
He whips through the door dancing.
I grab his ankle.

Stop. Look at me.
I took The Pills.
I tried to kill it.
I spit the words, then pause, probing his eyes.
What if it doesn't work?
What if it lives?

No problem, he says.
I'll pay half.
Let me know and
I'll write a check.
He turns up the radio
and dances again.

The deep cold leaves the air thick and still,
the sky dark at 2 p.m.
I am lost in a void.
I stare at him.
I do not know this man.

I walk out the door
carrying a life I cannot support.
Already feeling the anguish
of the months ahead.
Already wondering
if I will ever heal.

Three days later he calls.
I met a girl at the bank, he says.
I'm going to see her.

You're breaking the rules, I tell him.
Pick one.

Her.

Anger grows like the seed inside of me.
I go ice-skating and fall, crack my wrist.
I bolt for a warmer place to recover
and to hide.

In San Francisco my period is due.
I head downtown to the drugstore
and scan the tests.
A man approaches
and my trembling hand knocks them from the shelf.

I race to the counter, out the door, heart pounding.
Where are the goddamn bathrooms?
I cuss at the woman in the information booth.

I tear down the street, furious about the long walk.
I sit in the stall fumbling with the test
and pee in the wrong part.

I run
Back to the drugstore,
pulling a hat over my head
as I buy another test
and a Coke
because I have to pee again
Dammit.

I drink it running down the street, crying,
spilling it over my clothes.

Back in the stall,
the red line means positive.
My head falls to my lap
and I weep.

I avoid the piercing stares of the women
gathered outside my stall as I dash away,
grateful for the city madness
instead of the penetrating stillness
of Fairbanks.

I roam the streets for hours in a daze
then make the call.

It's me.
Silence.
I cannot speak.
I only weep, and he knows.
No problem, he says.
I'll write you a check.

II
I work frenetically,
dashing around the office.
My piercing pain and anger
have become energy.

After work I collapse
and I cry

and I succumb to the dizziness and sickness
of early pregnancy.

I feel the child every moment
as my body transforms to support it.
I am awed, mystified.
I feel a connection and a life force
more powerful than anything I have known.

The certainty of my decision
is an iron weight crushing my heart.
It is not a choice.
There are no options.

I struggle for a way to kill the child
without killing myself.
I cannot allow this life to grow and then harm it later.
I cannot wait six weeks for the abortion.
I swear I will die before then.
I'll never be able to do it, and I must.

Thinking too much.
Gotta stop thinking.
Gotta fill the time
to save me from myself.
I hate myself.
I hate myself for having sex,
for creating this inescapable mire.

At night I work a job on the phone
in a desperate attempt to dodge my own life.
I cannot forgive my mistake.

I cannot face the life I've created.
And so I run myself to exhaustion
so I won't feel
Anything.

I cannot sell on the phone.
It is a stupid job,
but when they fire me I am horrified.
My evenings are returned to me
and the time is a curse.

I cannot tell my family,
but I hear them.
God punishes sex before marriage.
It is sinful.
It is wrong.
Mom said so.
The church said so.
The teachers. The youth groups.
They all said so.

Stay here.
Stay here where it's safe.

My small Midwestern town wrote the rules
and I broke them.
I walked across the county line,
across the country.
A single woman alone in Alaska.
I carved out my own life.
I'm not like them.

But I am.
I carry the fear, the guilt, the shame.
I waited and I waited.
But then I had sex
Unmarried.

So they are right.
It was a sin, and God has punished me.
Sentenced with anguish.
I asked for it.

III
Weeks after the abortion
I am still bleeding.
I am scared and alone.
I have to talk.

My sister, six years older, became pregnant after college.
Under my mother's wrath and fury,
she kept the child
and married quietly, shamefully.

She knows.
She will understand.
I ask her for support.
But she screams into the phone.
How could you
when you weren't married?

It is my mother on the line.
It is not my sister.

I remember her, before her pregnancy.
Now she is gone.

I end the call.
I am still alone.

IV
A friend has betrayed my confidence.
Everyone knows. The whole town knows.
My personal struggle is gossip
and I am embittered.

The funding for my position has ended.
I have had it with my career of four years.
I have had it with the cold.
I have had it with all of them.

It is time to go.

I pull out a map and circle towns
down the west coast.
I'll go anyplace I can be anonymous.
Anyplace along the ocean.
Anyplace opposite Fairbanks.

My finger lands on Juneau.
No job. No friends.
Just ocean. Whales.
Two weeks later my truck is loaded.
I make the fourteen-hour drive to meet the ferry.

It's beautiful. Warm.
I am immersed in a new world,
and for weeks I forget everything.
I have erased my past.

But I cannot outrun the anger, shame,
and sadness that follow me.

The feelings fester and grow.
Eventually I am forced to look within
and acknowledge my own responsibility.
I've been beating myself up,
a constant diatribe running through my head.
I realize I have to confront the real enemy.
I have to take control of my abusive thoughts.

My mind knows I can enjoy sex without marriage.
My mind knows I made the right decision.
My mind knows I can make mistakes
and forgive
and let go.

But my heart is following rules
from someone else's game.
It is time to purge the voices
And fill my heart with reason and love
from my own experience.

Slowly, month by month
I catch those voices of judgment and anger
and I replace them with love and forgiveness.

I rebuild my life
as I rebuild my mind.

The light behind my eyes returns.
The gift of my child
is a depth of understanding, strength,
peace and forgiveness
in all areas of my life.

V
Two years later I am happy, settled,
my life replenished by the ocean.

But as the anniversary of the abortion approaches
I am plagued by nightmares.
I feel the pain of loss
and the soul of the child I let go.
I have accepted those feelings.
What surprises me
is the sudden return of shame and guilt.

In the dream my mother finds me
with blood on my dress.
She unleashes a fury upon me
and I am left crushed,
huddling in a corner like a frightened child.

Other dreams are not so clear.
Fleeting images of winter.
Frozen tears.
Often I remember nothing.
I only wake with a sense of terror.

The nightmares build over weeks.
On the day of the anniversary
my emotions overwhelm me.
I call my mother and tell her
what happened.
I tell her I need her support
and fear her judgment.

I am not granted absolution.
She explodes into a tirade
beyond my worst nightmares.
I am tried and convicted instantly.
I cut the call, then cry for hours.

A week later we try again.
I am desperate for acceptance and resolution.
But my mother cannot hear my anguish.
The conversation grows in absurdity and
our voices sharpen.
Again we are screaming.

She is thoughtless and cruel.
Yet the torrent of abuse grants me insight.
I see what I must overcome.
I will not lose myself like my sister.

We will not meet here.
We will never reach understanding.
But I will not allow my heart to be poisoned again.
I must forgive her and let go.

The nightmares subside
and I move on.

VI
Now I stand defending the right
with a new understanding and respect.
I guard my right to choose.
I guard my right to hurt.
I guard my right and the rights of others
to wrestle with the enormity of the choice
in full privacy.
I guard the right to suffer, to hit bottom
and come back up.

*Editor's Note: The author of has used a pseudonym to protect her privacy.

THE NECESSARY EVIL

Rochelle Moser

The necessary evil—that's about the most positive public opinion on abortion these days, even among some feminists. Of course I am well aware of the fire-and-brimstone approach to the issue; I walk past groups of anti-abortion protesters every day on my way into work at Planned Parenthood. Until last year, abortion was a purely political issue for me. My personal experience proved to be much different.

I had experienced some side effects from the birth control pill so I decided to try a diaphragm. For ten months it worked, although I would take a pregnancy test every month because I knew that the efficacy rates with a barrier method were much lower than with the Pill. Each month the pregnancy test was negative, so slowly I began to feel more confident about using a diaphragm.

The last time I requested a test, I knew something was wrong. My breasts were swollen and very tender, and I was tired all the time. I hadn't skipped my period yet, but I intuitively knew that I was pregnant. Nevertheless, I was shocked when my co-worker told me that my pregnancy test was positive, and that I was pregnant.

I had often played out a pregnancy scenario in my mind, trying to anticipate the various ways that I might react. I imagined feeling fear, disbelief, anxiety, and shame. But what I actually felt was joy. All the assumptions I had made about abortion crumbled. I thought there were only two ways of responding to an unplanned pregnancy: if the pregnancy was unexpected, but you were open to the idea, you were supposed to feel happy; if you did not want to have a child, you were expected to feel stressed, annoyed, and embarrassed. I knew immediately that I would have an abortion, but to my surprise, I felt immense joy and a connection to my body that I had never felt before.

I was fortunate to work at Planned Parenthood because it helped normalize the experience for me. Much of the societal shame surrounding the issue of abortion had dissipated, so I was free to genuinely respond to my pregnancy, without inhibition.

It felt like a dry well within me had tapped into a new water table. I felt this entity within me, flooding me with immense strength and love. For the first time in my life, I recognized the power of my body. For so long it had been this unfinished product. I was constantly trying to improve, but never quite satisfied with the results. When I discovered that I was pregnant, it hit me that my body actually "worked" and that I had had this incredible capability all along. As a result, I was able to let go of my intense hatred for my body and appreciate it for what it was. What a foolish waste of time and energy to fall prey to standards of beauty that promote the skeletal human hanger look. The wide spectrum of beauty suddenly revealed itself to me, and I noticed beautiful women everywhere, most of whom were waging their own body-hate wars, still unable to see their own bodies' resplendence.

While pregnant, there was also the feeling that I was never alone. I spent a lot of time lying on my bed with my hand on my belly letting the buzz of contentment vibrate through me. Experiencing pregnancy firsthand helped me to better understand pregnant women. I had always been puzzled by why anyone would go through the hell of pregnancy: the back strain, fatigue, hemorrhoids, incontinence, not to mention the birthing process. And to what end? So you could put your own dreams on hold, or more likely, give them up entirely? To a certain extent, I still feel this way. I am selfish and I know it. I want to travel the world and be a perpetual student. I know that, from my perspective, having a child would mean giving up many of my dreams, and until I am as joyful about the prospect of becoming a parent as I am about my other pursuits, I can't give a child what he/she deserves. But the pregnancy helped me to see why others would choose parenthood. My pregnancy experience struck a very basic primal chord within me, and I was amazed by the creation occurring within me. The piece that was the most amazing to me was the creative process itself, not the end result.

I also thought a lot about the sense of completion I was experiencing during that time. It became clear to me that my pregnancy symbolized the ideal family for which I had always yearned. I grew up in a chaotic family. There were many things I wanted from my parents that they were unable to provide. They did their best under the circumstances, but those elements that were lacking left holes in my psyche. As an adult, I had tried to fill those holes through subconscious role-playing: the mother searching for someone to nurture; the child aching for the unconditional love of a parent. This dynamic led to many frustrating and painful conflicts in my relationships, the details of which would require their own stories. Suffice it to say that I played that dynamic out with significant others, as I searched for the person who would fill those voids. For the short time I was pregnant, the desperate and frantic search stopped. I was both mother and child. I no longer sought completion from the outside because I possessed it within me.

I imagine a cup with holes spilling its contents. I would run around desperately trying to repair each hole but another would burst right next to it. When I became pregnant, the patchwork held and the water level stabilized. With the relief came replenishment and the ability to see the love that surrounded me in my friends and my partner. My cup was full.

Having an abortion is not always traumatic. If you can get beyond societal shame and expectation, you might find a message just waiting to be discovered. I never turned away from the fact that I would be ending a potential life. Facing and accepting that was the most important thing I could have done to prepare myself for my abortion. This might sound strange to some, but I actually talked with the being inside of me. I made peace with it. I knew that there was a reason for this pregnancy and it wasn't about becoming a mother. I truly believe this pregnancy came into my life to do exactly what it did: open me up to the strength I possessed, to crack open the rigid, limited way I was living my life, and to prove that everything I needed to nourish and repair those broken parts of my spirit, was there all along.[9]

PART II

VOICES FROM INSIDE THE ABORTION CLINIC

A CLINIC VISIT

Photographs By DeDe VanSlyke
With an Introduction by Krista Jacob

There are various stages a woman must go through before she obtains an abortion, most of which happen before she even enters the clinic. However, once she has made her decision and enters the clinic, she has several more steps to go through before she can undergo an abortion. Though there is some degree of variation among women's health clinic protocols, and considerable variation between early and late term procedures, the following images, taken by photographer DeDe VanSlyke, provide us with a small window into an abortion procedure. The pictures were taken at the Midwest Health Center for Women, an abortion provider in Minneapolis. The women in the photographs are volunteers, not patients, who agreed to participate in this photographic series for educational purposes. The photographs are a reenactment of the abortion procedure[10].

Each individual should check with their healthcare provider or healthcare clinic to find out more information about their specific protocols. For example, not all clinics have a counseling department and instead use patient educators to provide patient support and advocacy. In addition, there can be other significant differences.

After checking into the clinic, a woman is given a pregnancy test to confirm her pregnancy.

112 • Our Choices, Our Lives

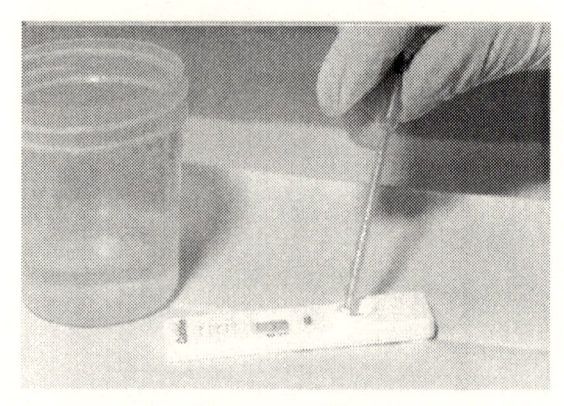

Pregnancy Test

Next, she has her blood drawn to check her Iron levels (Hematocrit), and to check her RH Factor. If a woman is RH Negative, she needs to receive an injection (shot) called Rhogam. Most women are RH Positive. This step is usually followed by a medical professional taking the patient's health history.

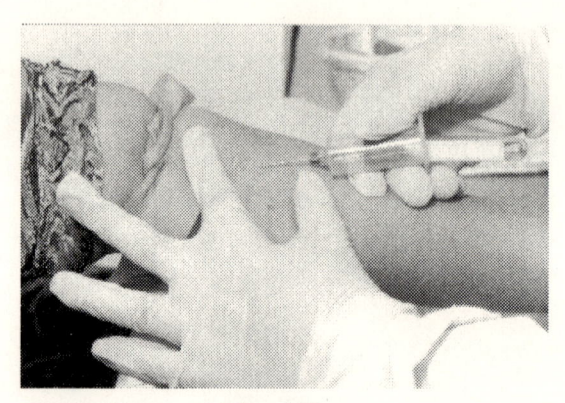

Blood Test

In most clinics, a medical professional performs an ultrasound. This procedure provides valuable information such as: how far along the pregnancy is, whether or not the patient is carrying multiple pregnancies, if the pregnancy is ectopic (stuck in the fallopian tubes), and whether or not the patient is having a miscarriage. This is also a time when some patients ask questions about embryonic or fetal development.

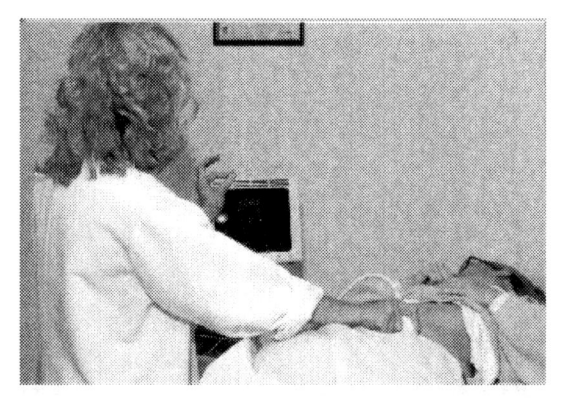

Ultrasound 1

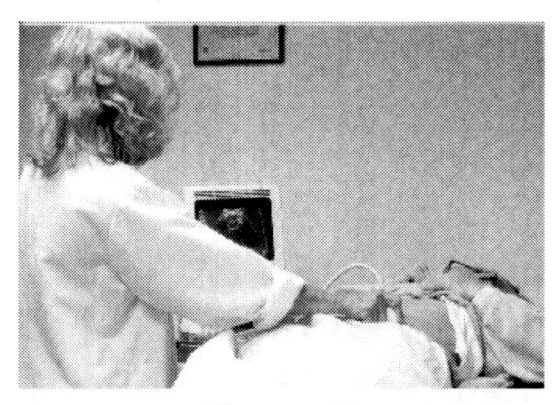

Ultrasound 2

Next, the patient meets with a counselor, patient educator, or nurse. The healthcare professional uses this time to explain the abortion procedure; answer questions; provide emotional support; assess the patient's decision and support network; assess the reasons for having an abortion;

provide birth control and referral information; and anything else the patient needs in preparation for the surgical procedure.

Counseling Session 1

Below, the counselor shows the patient a speculum, which is a medical instrument that is inserted into the vagina during the abortion procedure. This speculum is also used by physicians during annual pap smears and in various other gynecological procedures.

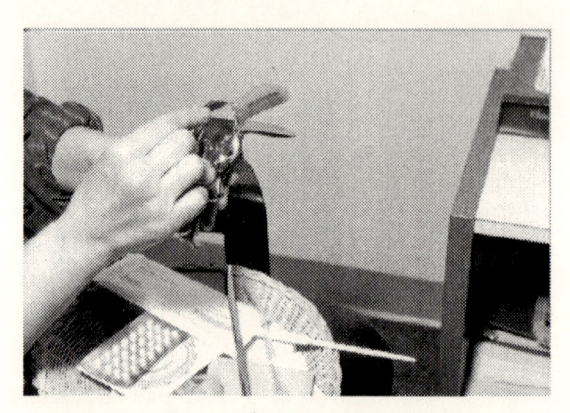

Counseling Session 2

Edited by Krista Jacob • 115

In the following photograph, a counselor explains the purpose of a dilator, a medical instrument used by the physician to dilate the cervix. The cervix is the opening into the uterus.

Counseling Session 3

A support person from the medical staff, usually a counselor, accompanies the patient through the surgery, and typically explains each step of the procedure as it is happening, assists with pain control, holds the patient's hand, or offers comfort in other ways. Sometimes patients prefer to remain quiet during the procedure, while others are more comfortable talking and asking questions.

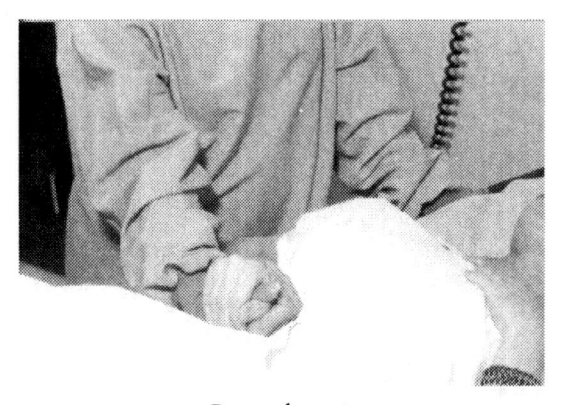

Procedure 1

Before the physician begins the abortion, the patient puts her feet in stirrups, which are located at the bottom of the exam table. As with any other medical procedure, the physician uses sterile surgical instruments to perform the abortion. After the speculum is inserted, the physician will numb the cervix with a local anesthetic.

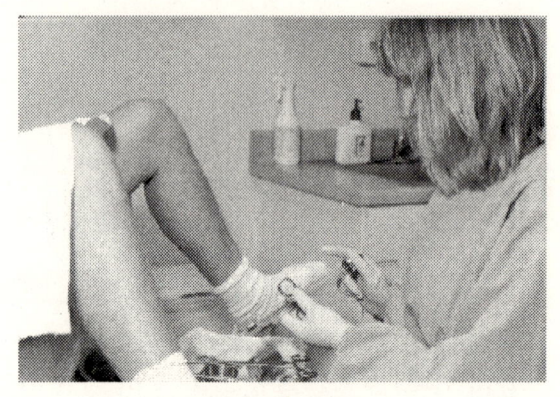

Procedure 2

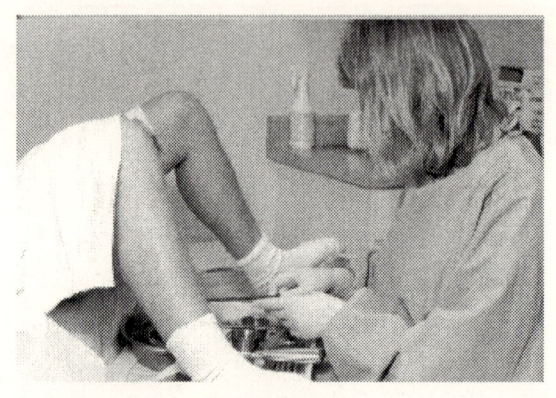

Procedure 3

To help stay relaxed and calm, patients are instructed to take slow, deep breaths.

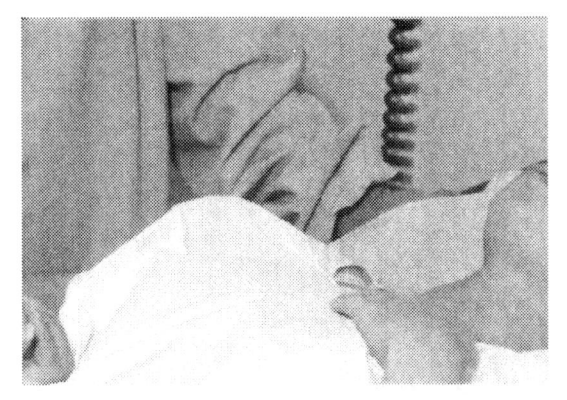

Procedure 4

The medical instrument below is called a cannula. The cannula is attached to the vacuum aspiration machine (see Procedure 6). Once the cervix is dilated, the cannula is inserted into the patient's uterus, and the pregnancy tissue and surrounding menstrual blood are emptied from the patient's uterus using gentle suction.

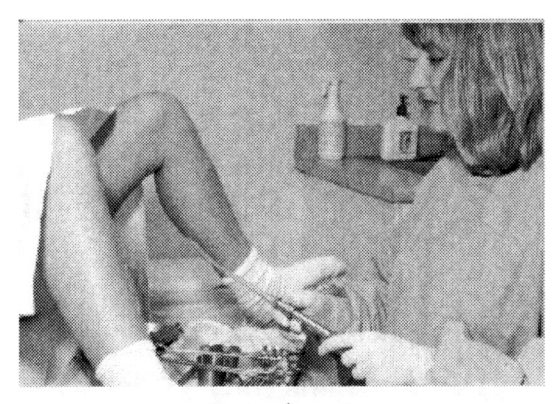

Procedure 5

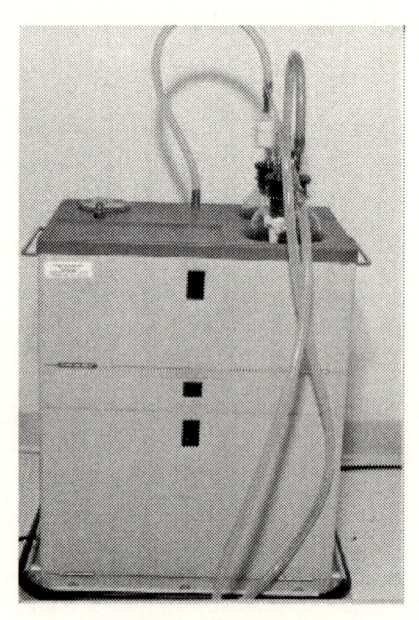

Procedure 6

For a first trimester and early second trimester abortion, the medical procedure itself takes about three to five minutes. The majority of the four-to six-hour clinic visit consists of the many steps a woman must go through before she has an abortion. Once the abortion is complete, the woman goes to a Recovery Room where she rests, receives further medical or birth control information, and is given a prescription for antibiotics. The Recovery Room nurse also monitors the woman's vitals and amounts of bleeding. Bleeding after the abortion is normal, and in some cases, can last as long as two weeks. Most women leave the Recovery Room about twenty minutes after their procedure. Once the procedure is complete, the majority of women express relief that they are no longer pregnant, and are free to move forward with their lives.

Edited by Krista Jacob • 119

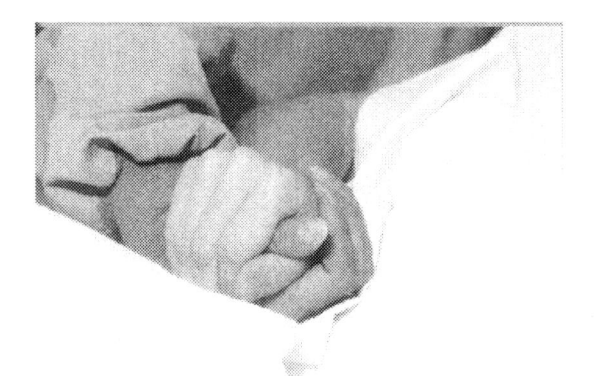

Procedure 7

BLESSING FOR THE ABORTIONIST'S HANDS

Elizabeth Moonstone*

Once the Wise Woman and the Midwife undid the pregnant possibility. With herbs and blessings they tended the women. Only rumors and warnings are left to us from that time. Recipes are lost. Pennyroyal is dangerous we are told and pregnant women are cautioned not to eat saffron. Now as an abortionist I have sterile instruments, knowledge of anatomy, modern drugs, a suction machine, and my hands.

Who blesses the Abortionist's hands?

> The spirits of the Grandmothers dream the Abortionist's hands.
> The spirits of the Midwives inform the Abortionist's hands.
> The spirits of the women who died in childbirth long for the Abortionist's hands.
> The spirits of the women burdened in life by too many children reach for the Abortionist's hands.
> The spirits of the children who died of starvation when the next child was born, cling to the Abortionist's hands.
> The spirits of the boys and girls not ready for children celebrate the Abortionist's hands.
> The spirits of the women whose lives are saved by abortions kiss the Abortionist's hands.
> All those Gods and Goddesses who love women and children, who love men, and who love life, bless the Abortionist's hands.

The Blessing

May my hands be deft and tender.
May I shake her hand with compassion.
May I feel the size and position of her uterus—lemon, orange, or grapefuit—between my hands.
May I numb her cervix painlessly, to ease her transition.
May I stretch the mouth of her uterus gently.
May I place the sterile plastic tube easily into her uterus.
In my abortionist's hands I hold the plastic-tipped wand attached to a suction machine.
May my hands move the wand skillfully, feeling the moment of emptying when her uterus clamps down.
May I not perforate the wall of her uterus or leave any pregnancy tissue behind.
May I not injure her in any way.
May my hands stay connected to my heart as I release this spirit and return this woman to herself and other possibilities.
Blessed be.

*Editor's Note: The author has chosen to use a pseudonym to protect her safety.

INTERVIEW WITH DR. CARRIE TERRELL

Rhonda Chittenden

Twin Cities' obstetrician-gynecologist Dr. Carrie Terrell has provided abortions services since 1997. Rhonda Chittenden briefly interviewed Dr. Terrell on her motivations to offer abortion services and on her perspective of the current "state of affairs" as a provider of surgical abortions.

RC: *What influenced your decision—personally, politically, and/or otherwise—to perform abortions?*
CT: During my teenage years, as I began to learn how political systems work, I was appalled to realize that nearly any person or group so motivated could engage the political process in an effort to limit a woman's access to abortion. This struck a deep chord in me that, I'm sure, influenced my decisions in schooling and career choices. During medical school, I chose my specialty to ensure that I would be trained and able to provide abortions.

RC: *How do you view your work: Do you see abortion as political, as a part of the greater movement for reproductive rights, or do you consider abortion to be simply another service on the menu of many services you provide as a gynecologist?*
CT: So many doctors have the ability and knowledge to provide abortions, but do not do so. For me, withholding these services is an example of "power over women" by limiting and thereby controlling women's reproductive decisions. Limiting abortion services—which in many cases is equivalent to not providing abortion services at all—reinforces women's roles as second-class citizens.

I view my work as an abortion provider as both medical and political. Surgical abortion is a safe, simple procedure. I feel it is an integral part of any Obstetrics and Gynecology practice. That said, by being an open and out provider, I hope to set a political and moral example to my colleagues.

RC: *What do you think are the most pressing concerns today related to abortion providers in the United States?*
CT: Our current most pressing concerns are the same concerns that women who may seek abortions are facing: the slow, constant etching away of abortion access, rights, and laws. Just as women cannot be assured safe, legal abortion services if access is limited or denied, I cannot be a provider unless I have the political and social system in place to support me.
RC: *What societal misconceptions are there about doctors who perform abortions, if any?*
CT: The largest societal misconception is that current abortion providers are gross old men who do nothing else. In reality, most providers manage a full practice that includes prenatal care, deliveries, gynecology, menopause care, and primary or preventive care. And many abortion providers are women.
RC: *What is the most challenging aspect of your work?*
CT: Since providing abortions is barely tolerated as part of my job, it is relegated to a "second job" or "moonlighting" status rather than as an integral part of my daily job responsibilities. Ensuring that I am available to provide this service puts extra demands on my already tight schedule and doesn't allow a proper forum for my abortion patients' phone calls, concerns, and complications. This is very frustrating.
RC: *Finally, what is the most rewarding aspect of your work?*
CT: Fortunately, this work is infused with automatic rewards. The patients are thankful for receiving the services and the clinic staff are wonderful to work with. At the end of the day, I feel I have accomplished something positive.[11]

DYSPLASIA

Dr. Virginia Bartholin*

Dysplasia "…abnormal growth or development (as of organs or cells)…" This term is used in medicine to describe pre-malignant growth of cells. It is the stage right before a cancer develops. I hope someday to write a book about my experiences in medical school and post-graduate training. If I ever do, I will entitle it "Dysplasia."

I have always been a feminist. At an early age I recognized various gender injustices throughout society, but I was never able to adequately verbalize my feelings. In high school the only exposure I had to so-called "feminists" were the few the media cared to spend time on—specifically those who blame women who have been raped and abused; and also tell women to pull themselves up by their bootstraps, giving no consideration to culturally sanctioned obstacles confronting women. It wasn't until college that a good friend helped to redirect my misguided Camille-Paglia-pseudofeminism into a more Andrea-Dworkin-Gloria-Steinem-Susan Faludi-type of feminism. It was then that I became pro-choice.

I always wanted to be a doctor. Why, you ask? Because I wanted to help people. I got over this delusion once I was in medical school, but that is a different subject. Now I lie somewhere in limbo between trying to reconcile the altruistic hope of helping others and the selfish desire to take care of myself and my family.

I am proud to call myself a feminist, which, in my opinion, by definition means that I am pro-choice. It wasn't until I read the June 1995 issue of Ms. Magazine that I was moved to make a commitment to provide abortions. Reading this issue of Ms. was a life changing event for me. My medical school, predominately White and located in the South, was not amenable to discussion of certain issues related to reproductive health. We once had a guest speaker from Planned Parenthood who gave a lecture on various birth control methods, Sexually Transmitted Infections (STIs), family planning, and the morning-after pill. Before this doctor even set foot on our campus, the letters of protest were distributed. The three minutes allocated for him to speak about the morning-after pill were enough to send the conservative-White-male-Christians into a hypertensive, tachycardic rage. They made vitriolic remarks, both about the speaker and about abortion, and about anyone who dared challenge their anti-choice crusade.

Their obsession with humanizing the embryo/fetus was pathological, using phrases like "murdering precious life." Yet, they were unwilling to see the glaring contradictions between their anti-choice beliefs and their support of the death penalty ("let them fry") and their anti-gun-control politics. Ironically, physicians see firsthand the consequences of the overabundance of guns. These men, like so many other anti-choice people, used the rhetoric of life, morality, and murder only when it suits their opinions. It's scary to realize that these narrow-minded, abusive students are now practicing physicians. Imagine how they treat women (and their partners) who inquire about pregnancy options. Even then, several of them stated that they believed the birth control pill to be immoral and that they would not prescribe it in their practice. Instead, they would preach abstinence.

This dangerous anti-abortion bias was not limited to a handful of misguided students. In my Obstetrics and Gynecology class, spontaneous abortions were referred to as "miscarriages," an incorrect medical term, but clearly less controversial. Further, elective abortions were not even mentioned, let alone taught. As a doctor interested in women's health care, I feel that my medical education was severely lacking in this regard. Their approach to this issue was not medically objective but rather served as a transmitter of, at best, their ambivalence about reproductive freedom and, at worst, their anti-choice bias.

Now, I am in my first year of residency. I did not go into Obstetrics and Gynecology mainly because I don't want the added responsibilities, erratic hours, malpractice issues, and so on. I can still provide abortions, although it is a bit more difficult to do so. I am in the process of observing and learning the procedure. In fact I have done a few abortions already. The first time I observed an abortion it was not a horrific scene (as the anti-choice factions would have you believe), but rather a clean, efficient, dignified procedure.

The procedure itself is simple, and it is safe when done by a properly trained physician. Conversely, if the person performing the abortion is not well trained, the possible complications are lethal. This is one of many reasons why the fact that elective abortion was not even *discussed* during my medical education is so dangerous. If any students wanted to actually learn the abortion procedure, they were forced to seek out, and sometimes with a lot of difficulty, someone who might know someone who might be able to help them find someone who knows of someone who does the procedure. Get the picture?

Now that I have relocated to the Midwest, I have a few more, and I mean only a few more, opportunities. A doctor who performs elective abortions in my community has taken me under his (very skilled) wing and is giving me the training I need. I am grateful to this man for many reasons, but mostly because he is a good teacher, and his training is making me more confident in both my skills and my politics. He risks his life daily by providing this procedure to women. He truly is a feminist. With the exception of this doctor and the handful of others who perform abortions and support doctors who perform abortions, the medical field itself is complicit in the deaths, the murders, the suicides and anything else that has resulted from this lack of healthcare training. It reminds me of the slogan: If you aren't part of the solution, you are part of the problem. I know that as a feminist physician, I want to be part of the solution.

*Editor's Note: The author has chosen to use a pseudonym to protect her safety.

PAPER-CLOTHED STRANGERS

Jennifer New

Jadine, is that her name? Why can't I remember her name? There is her bulk, her blues, her weariness. She reminded me of a large, scuffed suitcase that for years had been filled with other people's stuff. She was entrusted with the safe-keeping of their dreams, their wrong doings, their children, their illnesses. Forty-four years old and patiently exasperated, she muttered, "I didn't think this could still happen." Her voice was tired. This was just one more damned awful thing she had not been intending to have to deal with, but here she was—dealing.

She stared at the ceiling. Occasionally she closed her eyes, lightly. She tried to smile or nod at us. Hers was the lengthiest abortion I've seen. I really don't know how long we were all in tiny Room Four at the end of the hall. It was a warm summer evening, and with five of us in there the temperature rose. Through it all, people were prodding at her body. One doctor inserted a saline drip in her arm to keep her blood pressure up and to hydrate her. At Jadine's feet, the clinic director and another doctor, pale with concern, were tensely discussing whether to proceed. Jadine was more than twelve weeks along, twelve weeks being the maximum stage for which this clinic was equipped.

Across from the doctor, holding the saline drip up by Jadine's head, was me. A novice advocate, I was telling her to breathe, to hang on, though Jadine had obviously been breathing and hanging on with considerable tenacity for a long while. I wiped her forehead with a cool cloth. Trying to equal the strength of her grip, I held her hand. Later, I arranged the heating pad under her broad back.

I had done this for many women and nearly all were grateful. But Jadine was one of the few who was almost embarrassed by the kindness of these simple acts. She had held so many hands herself, children and grandchildren. For someone to do these things for her—whisper words of support, remove the cloths dampened by her sweat and blood—this was such a surprise. She didn't say much to me, but the humbleness of her thanks expressed its depth. Later, waiting outside for a cab, both of us exhausted and the night quietly warm, she directed her gaze at me and then away to some thought, perhaps of a prior touch or of tomorrow's work that would not wait for her to take the rest she really needed.

The experience of holding a stranger's hand during an abortion is a powerful one. A piece of your self is taken on by them, just as you take in their pain, relief, tears, and nervous laughter. Standing guard next to paper-clothed examination tables, I have been closer to more women than in every locker room and slumber party of my past. It is an odd bond that is made. One woman so exposed, the other there only to attend to her needs. You lie on your back, feet in stirrups, a doctor between your legs, instruments prodding inside, all extracting this small piece of you. No matter how patient and well-intentioned the others in the room are, you are bare, vulnerable. Scars are exposed. Your underwear, soft and worn, rests in a small pile on a chair. Your socks and toes stick up into someone's face. Laughing when you are afraid, you sob later with relief.

It all comes out so oddly here in this small cupboard of a room with these strange, concerned faces. This sliver is all they will know of you. They won't know that you balance your checkbook neatly each month or that you once read *War and Peace* in a week. These people, smelling clean and unfamiliar, might learn, because your body gives it away, that you've injected yourself with drugs or that you had a Caesarian. But those other things that make you whole, they won't know those. Now you are a body on a table covered with thin paper—a conglomeration of pulse and temperature, your family's cancer history, the date of your last period. Right now you are a woman who has decided to lie on this table, to go on with her life in a changed way, and these are the people accompanying you through the physical trials of that decision.

I too have lain on the table, my legs in stirrups, a mild sedative pulsing through my system, leaving a soft blur. The faces are fuzzy; I could never pick out the doctor or even the advocate who was there with me. I vaguely recall the chill of the speculum, and the quick fist of pain that was the cramping. But these are all physical memories. Afterward in the recovery room (how did I get there? did I fly?), I peered at the city. And though I have a mental snapshot of a gray, cold day dotted with European steeples and bare trees, this is all wrong because it was September and about eighty degrees outside.

When it was finished and I was dressed, the check was written and the receipt pressed between the pages of *The Day of the Locust* (where I found it two years later during a move), I probably said thank you. Almost all women for whom I have advocated have thanked me when it was over. It's odd how this makes you feel when you are there to assist. Often I will want to say, "No, thank you." Thank you for your patience, your nerves, your warmth. Thank you for revealing yourself.

Now and then, a woman will drop an unpolished stone in your lap, a memory or a dream, something she has held against herself warm and private all these years. And now, after you have held her hand and wiped away vomit from her mouth, now as you move the heating pad under her back, she tells you: "You are the only one who knows this happened. I couldn't tell my boyfriend because we're breaking up. None of my friends would approve. Just you." And so you put this responsibility in your pocket and try to carry it safely through whatever voyage it may be on. I have had women tell me of physical abuse, of failed friendships, of dreams unfulfilled. Momentarily I wonder why they have chosen me. I hope that it is not because there is no one else, though, sadly, I think this is usually the case. I must take care. I must try to remember.

At parties I hesitate to talk to unknown women, checking for any sign of familiarity. I fear someone pausing and squinting her eyes at me: "Don't I know you?" I have been around so many abortions that it seems to me that almost every woman has had one. It is not shameful; it is something that happens. Have sex, get pregnant—simple equation. For a woman to get through her entire life without a single unwanted pregnancy demonstrates an amazing degree of self-respect, emotional health, and just plain luck to which few of us are privy. An abortion seems to signal for many women that something is askew, that we need to make changes. This chance for alterations, the prevention of more serious ills, has always been for me the most formidable element of abortion.

But other people don't immediately see it this way. I have spoken to some of my closest friends about their abortions. Even with me, whom they know to be caring about the subject, their tones are hushed, the pauses long. This is wrong. You are weak. These sentiments are common and firmly intact, no matter what a woman's politics are. It is hard to shake them away and to replace them with visions of prevention, future and hope. Yes, these friends always include some positive outcomes in their accounts. Needed changes were made. They learned that only they can care for themselves. They gained respect for the power of their bodies. But these are afterthoughts to a story that is scattered with self-blame and guilt.

Recently, I was sitting in traffic in a suburb far from the clinic. A woman crossed right in front of me. Where had I seen her? She was wearing a Denny's restaurant uniform, and I recalled a particular woman and her boyfriend for whom I had advocated. They had impressed me with the unity and tenderness with which they approached the abortion. It was indeed her, looking happy and confident, totally unaware that someone who had been intimately involved in an hour of her life sat just feet away, watching her cross safely.

I could have sat next to the woman who had advocated for me in a restaurant or on a plane. Without doubt I have been on the same bus or in the same movie theater as some of the women for whom I've cared. Our paths cross gently, without our knowing. We help and we receive help in return. Perhaps I will see Jadine again. I would remember her face, I think.

Editor's Note: Originally appeared in Salon.com, on October 8, 1997.

CLINIC TESTIMONY

Carla Vogel
Interfaith Memorial Service, Temple Israel, Minneapolis, Minnesota
Remembering Dr. Barnett Slepian killed October 23, 1998, in Buffalo, New York

I have been a Reproductive Health Counselor/Abortion Counselor at Midwest Women's Health Center for over two and a half years. When I tell people what I do, I usually get the same questions and comments: "What's it like?" "I bet it's stressful." "Doesn't that work burn you out?"

Sometimes the only way I can describe it is to say that working at an abortion clinic is like eating a really rich piece of chocolate cheesecake, it's so rich you can only eat one bite at a time. Let me give you a taste.

Clinic days are usually four to six hours long and within that time I am privy to every human emotion: pain, grief, joy, fear, anger, laughter, rage, and despair. Within that four to six hours, I also see, smell, and touch many of the bodily fluids that connect us all: blood, sweat, tears, urine, and vomit.

Counseling sessions are usually twenty minutes long, and within that twenty minutes I am a witness to a myriad of stories from women of all ages, walks of life and cultures; the fourteen year old, the forty-six-year old divorced woman, the factory worker, the corporate executive, the Native American, African American, Latina, European American, Asian American, Hmong, Russian, Somalian, Ethiopian, Bosnian, Chinese, and so on. In that twenty minutes each woman bares a piece of her soul. I see her shame, fear, spiritual struggle, relief, grief, and I see her compassion.

Then there is the abortion itself, which takes five minutes. Within that five minutes, that timeless five minutes that can seem like an eternity, I am a hand-holder, a breath coach, a tear wiper. I help each woman push through one of the most powerful and painful five minutes of her life.

For me that five minutes is holy. I believe that within that short time, the mysteries of birth and death come full circle, and that the potential of life is transformed.

Then there's my favorite part of the day. The staff breaks, which can be a five-minute coffee break, a cigarette break, a fifteen-minute run to McDonalds, Subway, or Nankin or the happy hour at T.J. Fridays when the day is over. This is where we, the staff, let our hair down, where we swap stories about our children, our problems, our love lives, our dreams. We laugh, we complain, we argue, we cry. We bond.

That bond is so thick. See, when you work in an abortion clinic, whether as a lab tech, doctor, nurse, counselor, front desk worker, director, or financial administrator, the job demands that you give your whole self—your mind, body, heart, and soul.

On those long days, the days that I feel like quitting, I sometimes imagine that the clinic is surrounded by all the ancestors of the abortion movement. All the women and men who fought and died for this cause; they inspire me and give me courage.

When I am not an abortion counselor, I am a Storyteller. I just returned from Mt. Zion Synagogue where I was telling Chanukah stories to children. One of the themes of Chanukah is to continue fighting for what you believe in, even if you feel powerless and endangered. So it is in the spirit of Chanukah and Dr. Slepian that we keep fighting for what we believe in, and that we keep the light burning.

THE BREEZE IN THE WAITING ROOM

Jenny Higgins

Today the waiting room across from the lab is, as usual, stone silent, save for the flipping of a few outdated magazines or the sound of a talk show on the television with the volume turned down. How odd, I have often thought, to be sitting in a room full of women who are complete strangers, yet who all share something incredibly private and sacred. Often they'll be sitting in there for two, sometimes three hours, alone, yet at the same time, together in their misery. Funny.

Occasionally, a distraught patient will stick her head into the lab and ask if there is a room where she can be alone. "I'm sorry, that's all we've got," is all I can answer. These are the ones who are shocked when they're brought into Recovery; even after the procedure, the patients are herded together again, sprawling, drugged, and exhausted, across couches and chairs. Only Sally works in there, and she doesn't talk much. Maybe someday I'll get up the courage to ask her if the women's eyes meet any more in Recovery than they do in the waiting room.

A woman comes into the lab asking for a glass of water, a bit loopy from Valium. "Is it all right if we open the door of the waiting room so we can smoke?" she asks. "I asked the others if they would mind and they said no." I look at Amy, who is taking a blood pressure. "Both security guards are on today," she says, "and the door opens out into the back parking lot. It should be fine."

"Sure, go ahead," I tell the woman, and she wobbles a bit as she turns and heads back into the waiting room. When, a moment later, a warm breeze from the open door skims through the lab, I suddenly remember how gorgeous it is outside—a sunny and clear June morning. The breath of air winds seductively around my neck and mingles with the hairs on my arms, sending a warm shiver over my skin. "God, that feels nice," I announce to no one in particular. Amy answers anyway, with an exaggerated sigh. "We've gotten too god-damn used to that stale crap from the air conditioner, if you ask me." She moves into the doorway to feel the breeze across her face. "Mmmm." I turn my attention back to the charts, but in a moment she says quietly, "Jenny, come here a minute. You've got to see this."

I move next to her in the doorway and peer into the waiting room When I see how the dull painted walls have been ignited with sunlight, it occurs to me that the clinic does not have a single window. Then I notice that all the patients have crowded around the open door, letting the breeze dance and sway on their closed eyelids. They are so close that many of their arms are touching, and one woman actually rests her head on the shoulder of the woman next to her. Someone has turned the television off, so the only sound is the light rustling of leaves from the young birch trees bordering the ugly back parking lot.

"Where the hell is that breeze coming from?" Betsy demands as she rounds the corner from her office. She looks in surprise to the open door, then to Amy and me. Amy shrugs sheepishly and whispers, "a couple of them wanted to smoke, and it was so nice outside…" Betsy narrows her eyes and heads toward the group of patients. "I'm sorry, ladies, but you'll have to close the door. It just isn't safe." As she shuts the door, one last lovely gust blows through the room, then settles into the carpet. I watch the women go back to their seats and pick up their magazines, the buzz from the fluorescent lights seemingly louder than before.

WHY WE ARE SENDING YOU HOME

Shari Aronson

I don't remember your name. I wouldn't recognize you if you passed me on the street nor got into the same elevator. No specific hairstyle, skin tone, or eye color emerges when I try to picture you. When I think of you, you are African American, eighteen and pregnant for the first time; these are the details I read off your medical chart before I called you in from the clinic's waiting room for counseling.

You move your eyes and body away from my "hello" as if to say "no" before any questions are asked. You sit down in my office. My arm hairs bristle in the chill of the air conditioning. I figure I'll start talking, warm us up.

I hold instruments, point to the diagram of female anatomy, mime the doctor's actions of the insertion of the speculum and its movements all the way through the suctioning. I tell you that I'll be with you during the procedure. If there is anything I can do to make you more comfortable, I say, let me know. I consider saying, "And beneath your seat you will find a flotation device," to acknowledge the ridiculousness of you, and me, and comfort attempting to be in the same room. Me, the White middle-class rookie abortion counselor trying to run down the checklist of Doing Good. You, occasionally glancing in my direction as if I were an unwanted salesperson who showed up on a Sunday at eight a.m. on your porch. You seem to be waiting for me to pause for breath so you can shut the door.

The clock ticks off a third minute. By the time the little hand moves another six inches, I need to find out why you are choosing abortion, how you are doing emotionally with the decision, what systems of coping you have in place, and then cover birth control and aftercare instructions. Having failed to build the quick rapport necessary for asking intimate questions, now I must ask you the intimate questions.

I strive to formulate a tone of voice that is warm, genuine, not cloying or prying. If I could just compose a sound with words that magically elicits response.

"Why do you want an abortion?" I ask. Your chin arcs up off your chest dragging your gaze to meet mine. I focus on opening, my eyes, my attitude, my being eager to make even a synapse twitch of connection. You speak.

"I want to break the chain of single mothers in my family." Yes! We are playing on the same team and our side of the scoreboard is glowing. Then you add, "I don't want you to kill my baby. But no one will tell me the options."

"…kill…baby…" red lights flicker and a buzzer hiccups. I show you brochures about adoption, free prenatal medical clinics and no-cost parenting support services. You repeat.

"I don't want you to kill my baby. But no one will tell me my options." The clock hands whir and wrestle with the effort of moving to the next minute like a windup toy that fell over on its back. The little boxes I must check off on the counseling form stare up at me.

"The firmness of the patient's decision was assessed:
>Definite in thinking and feeling.
>Conflicted thinking, but made decision without coercion.
>Ambivalent, will think it over and reschedule."

I am supposed to pick the statement that fits you. I fumble to make the appearance that the conversation is continuing, while part of my brain slips into a back chamber to scan archival files. I'm still looking at you, I'm probably still gesturing. But what I see is a bullet-point sampler of counseling training.

"Conflicted patients seem to have the most problems during the abortion. Cramps wring their bodies as viciously as their doubts. Failure to stay still on the table and take control of breathing raises the risks of medical complications."

"If a woman holds the clinic responsible for doing an abortion to her when she did not want one, the clinic becomes vulnerable to litigation. One major lawsuit could easily deplete the finances of a small non-profit clinic. The loss of our clinic could reduce the access to safe low-cost abortions for thousands of women."

"If the patient can't convince us that she wants the abortion and she will be okay after an abortion, to let her through could possibly endanger the well-being of all involved."

The old-timers on the clinic staff, the nurses who worked with abortion pre-legal in the underground, find the concept of indecision absurd. Before 1973, women had to hunt down a doctor, a clinic, or even a country to terminate a pregnancy. Back then, a woman knew that to go through the procedure would be risking her life. Supposedly, once a patient made it to the door of the abortion provider, she was sure of the decision to go through the abortion.

You found our number listed in the yellow pages under Abortion. You, too, had to struggle: dig up hundreds of unbudgeted dollars, wade through protesters and combat fear of bleeding, pain and God. But, legal and professional medical standards protect your rights. The freedom to choose is priceless, but the options can be overwhelming.

The first patient I ever counseled hopped off the table just after the doctor put in the speculum. In the counseling session, she had vehemently said that she wanted nothing to do with her boyfriend nor his child and was absolutely determined to end both relationships. Then she went out into the lobby to wait for her turn to see the doctor. The boyfriend showed up. As she waited for me to call her name, he talked about Jesus and cried in her lap. She was the fourteenth patient on the list. By the time I called her in to the procedure room, the boyfriend had had hours with which to work. Sitting in the paper gown, feeling the cold metal of the instrument push at her skin, suddenly she reversed all her previous declarations. She announced that she was not going to go through the abortion and instead was going to get married.

I was shocked. Everything had seemed so clear at 10:00 a.m. But at 2:15 p.m., the patient was planning her wedding and I was worrying that the doctor suspected me of not knowing what I was doing. By 2:30 p.m. I wondered, too.

You say you will definitely regret having an abortion. You would like to raise this child. But, you add, no one in your life, not your family nor the male involved in your pregnancy, cares about you. So you might as well just "kill the baby." Your movements and words lash out and jerk, like an animal daring a predator to pounce.

I wish I had a time machine to take you back five minutes before conception. You could choose to use or switch birth control or even elect not to have sex. I suppose that would just be another decision.

I reach for the form marked "Why We Are Sending You Home." I say, "I'm not telling you that you can't have an abortion at this clinic today. You can go to another clinic or come back to our clinic another day for indecision counseling." Then I add referrals for low-cost therapists.

Your fingers brush over the pamphlets about available resources that I put in front of you. Your mouth jumps and wiggles and out stammers bits of words. Your shoulders heave up, they drop down. There's a moment when it appears as if you might grip onto the side of the chair until your muscles explode. Instead, you release. You rise to your feet and move to the door. You don't look back.

I don't have a window from which I can see your departure. I imagine you passing the protester who stands in front of the clinic on the sidewalk. She smiles and gives you a photo of a fetus.

Of all places, you never expected an abortion clinic to reject you. I bet the protester would be surprised, too. Don't we eagerly lure innocent mothers-to-be into our lair to dance in the blood of the unborn and the piles of blood money? Did abortion activists envision your scene while fighting for and defending women's reproductive rights?

You are the first person I send home as an abortion counselor. You are not the last. Some women leap up and say, "Okay," and start collecting their belongings before I can finish with the Sending You Home Spiel, as if they are relieved someone is telling them they cannot do what they don't really want to.

Others resist. A woman sighs, her pitch jumps up or down a few notes. Even if her husband/boyfriend/mother would agree to raising another child, she knows she herself is not ready/able/willing to carry this pregnancy to term. The patient does what she needs to with her posture, voice, and face to convince the counselor that in this moment, compared to the previous several, she speaks the truth. She wants the abortion.

When a patient leaves before the procedure, the counselors cross her number off the list and write next to the black line "Undecided." Many who leave the clinic undecided return the next day or the following week. The counselor then must determine, what in those extra hours brought the woman back here?

As far as I know, you do not come back to our clinic to terminate your pregnancy. Maybe you go home and talk to your mother. For the first time in your life she offers to help. Maybe you run away. If you are still alive, at least one day a year, you celebrate your child's birthday, grieve for a heavy stain on your heart, or work to bury it. My guess now is as good as the guess I made that day.

Split seconds of perception and gut feelings crescendo into a yes or no. No, you do not demonstrate the skills or support necessary to cope with an abortion. No, you do not demonstrate the skills or support necessary to cope with adoption or motherhood. Which box do I check?

You say you want to break the chain of single mothers in your family. I want to help you reach your goal. I took this job to carry out such dismantling-the-oppressor missions.

Yet, with one flick of a form I turn you away from the abortion clinic, pregnant. And you send me home, undecided.

HEAT WAVE

Jenny Higgins

When I'm angry now I think of the retarded girl
Who came into the abortion clinic last summer,
Her nose running even though we were stuck
In the middle of July, her eyes distant
And distorted through the thick thick lenses
Of her glasses, her mother gingerly fingering her hair
As though it weren't greasy and stringy with oil.

It was her stepfather, Betsy told me, her stepfather
Who climbed on top of her that night, as he had
On countless other nights, clamping down her mouth
With his palm—not like she could have tried
To scream anyway. Her glasses weren't broken,
I imagine, because her mother placed them
On the night table before tucking the girl into bed.

On the table, she can't control the flow
Of blood any more than the flow from her nose,
And she stares vacantly through her glasses
At the ceiling as it leaks down the underside of her thigh
And onto the sterile drape pinned beneath her ass
Like a painter's drip sheet. She'll bleed
For two weeks, maybe three, the used pads
Pungent and rank in this ungodly July heat.

JUST ANOTHER DAY AT WORK

Kathleen George Kearney

Martyrdom is not encouraged, yet the willingness to risk physical harm, and even death, is acknowledged as sometimes necessary.
Sharon Welch, *A Feminist Ethic of Risk*.

there are those minutes,
rare and precious and
full of enfleshment,
"There's a bomb threat."
when we can choose
between life and death
"Get out and save yourself while you can."
and live again.
"I would die for this cause, I really would."
i pause only a moment.
"If I die,
i decide not to pray.
I'll die doing something I love."
i walk away.
the next morning,
after a night of
sweating into sheets
and the far-away sound of a worried mother crying,
i return to my holy ground,
find the clinic standing
and still receiving
the tired   the hungry   the full   the empty   the bold.
A protester clutches her sign

I Knew You in the Womb
and walks into me with flat, dull eyes:
"There's blood on your hands."

I PREPARE THE FIFTEEN-YEAR-OLD

Jenny Higgins

"You're going to be out of here in eight minutes,"
I say as I lift tense legs into the stirrups
For the sixth time today. Silent
Since I walked her in from the waiting room,

Her body hasn't loosened
with my usual chatter: the doctor's nice,
How much bleeding to expect, no swimming
For at least two weeks—the bacteria.

But now, as I watch her eyes graze
The Impressionist prints tacked to the ceiling
Above her, her small heart-shaped face hard
And impassive, I realize it's not information

She needs. Though flesh is hard to feel
Through latex gloves, I touch her forearm
And ask about the tiny golden angel
Pinned to the neck of her T-shirt.

From my mother, she says, and the firm,
Set line of her chin finally gives, crumpling
Up to meet her bottom lip as she lets out a cry.
The tears stream down the steep sides of her cheeks

Into her ears, and her small breasts
Heave and shudder with the sobs.

Jesus, this is hard, I think,
To wish I could erase the pain and the past,

To wish, even though I know nothing
Of her but unraveled courage, that it was my body
On the table, not hers, my womb to be scraped
Clean, my clothes to go home stained

With the unrelenting memory of blood.
I squeeze the young girl's hand
and whisper, "I know you can make it."

DEBBIE, WHO STANDS OUTSIDE A CLINIC EVERY SATURDAY

Kathleen George Kearney

your chapped fingers curl over the signboard,
ABORTION KILLS CHILDREN
joints stiff in the cold wind of February in Minnesota.
ABORTION: THE AMERICAN HOLOCAUST
pamphlets clenched tight in one fist,
THINGS YOU SHOULD KNOW BEFORE YOU HAVE AN ABORTION
sprayed with pictures of blood and dismemberment
WHAT THEY WON'T TELL YOU IN THE CLINIC
like Vietnam, like machine gun fire.
THE MIRACLE OF LIFE
standing on the edge of the clinic property,
THIS IS A HOUSE OF DEATH
you yell at diabetics needing insulin,
DON'T GO INTO THE KILLING CENTER
pensioners with yearly check-ups,
MURDER SHOULDN'T BE A CHOICE
schoolchildren going for flu shots.
WE'RE HERE TO HELP YOU
a young woman walks quickly down the sidewalk.
PLEASE TAKE THIS INFORMATION
you see her eyes. you know.
PLEASE DON'T KILL YOUR BABY
rushing upon her,
THIS DOCTOR HURTS WOMEN
you pounce, thrust, reach, do battle
AT THREE WEEKS YOUR BABY HAS A HEARTBEAT

all to give her the same salvation you hide yourself in,
AT FOUR WEEKS YOUR BABY CAN FEEL PAIN
the holy righteousness that keeps you safe.
AT FIVE WEEKS YOUR BABY IS FULLY FORMED
you have practiced this for years,
IT'S A CHILD, NOT A CHOICE
in church, in Pro-life Action meetings, in your silent bed.
WE HAVE FINANCIAL HELP AVAILABLE
and she has torn up your literature,
THINK ABOUT WHAT YOU'RE DOING
cursed you loudly,
THEY'LL LIE TO YOU IN THERE
shoved you down to the rough pavement,
JESUS LOVES YOU
and marched away.
I'LL PRAY FOR YOU

HONORING PLEASURE

Sue Schlangen

For the past ten years, I have been talking, writing, and thinking about almost every aspect of sexuality imaginable. I've conducted homophobia/biphobia/sexphobia lectures routinely for a period of five years. My master's degree in Human Development focused exclusively on issues of sexuality such as homophobia, biphobia, and sexphobia.

All these years, I have been thinking about a wide range of sexual issues, such as gay/lesbian sexuality, bisexuality, S/M (sadomasochism), polyamory, teen sexuality, transgender issues, prostitution, sexual healing, masturbation, and sexual shame. There are other topics I have been thinking about as well, but one topic that seemed to escape my attention was abortion. In February 1999, I started working as a Reproductive Health Counselor at a clinic where abortions, as well as other reproductive health services, are provided. The issue of abortion as it relates to sexuality has now taken center stage for me.

While I was not surprised by how difficult a decision abortion can be for women, I was surprised by the number of women I counseled who had expected to feel bad or guilty about having the abortion, when, in fact, they did not feel that way at all. When this issue comes up in the counseling session, I acknowledge the many judgments against abortion by certain segments of society. I often mention the protesters outside the clinic (if she doesn't) to illustrate for her one of the obstacles she had to experience just walking into the clinic. I tell her that half of my job, sometimes, is dealing with the negative atmosphere that can be created by those kinds of judgments. Given all of this judgment, I do not minimize the fact that the decision to have an abortion can be difficult. Still, I question why these women, who basically are comfortable with their decision to have an abortion, are being pressured to feel bad about it.

Often there is no clear-cut answer to why there is an unintended pregnancy. I've observed at the clinic that someone can use birth control perfectly and still become pregnant. Everyone is different, so what works for one person does not necessarily work for someone else. But what is clear is that the unplanned pregnancy came as a result of sex. If it was not coerced sex, then often sex comes out of an attempt to feel closeness and pleasure.

Sex and sexuality do not always go as planned. Sex and relationships are fluid, moving, changing phenomena. Even if someone has only one partner in their lifetime, sex does not usually stay stagnant and unmoving even with that one person. Intimacy may deepen, skill may change and, one hopes, become enhanced. Interest in what to try may change for one or both persons. Sometimes what the people involved choose to do sexually may be pleasurable, and sometimes not. And, in some situations, an unintended pregnancy may occur.

The only way to completely avoid an unplanned pregnancy is not to have penis-in-vagina sex at all. It is ironic to me that often the same people who don't think abortion is acceptable are also the same people who do not think masturbation or same-sex sexuality are acceptable either, both being sexual expressions where no unintended pregnancy could result, and therefore, no abortion. Of course, there are other sexual practices that would also not result in a pregnancy, such as oral and anal sex. These sexual practices seem to find judgment as well from the individuals who would advocate for abstinence, unless it meets their standards for what is morally right and acceptable.

What I would say to the abstinence advocates and what I do say to the women who come to the clinic for abortions, is that we each have a right to be sexual. We have a right to be sexual with ourselves, with another person, with someone of the same gender, someone of the opposite gender, more than one person in a lifetime, and in all the unique ways that we might choose to be sexual in any given situation. We have a right to determine what is desirable for ourselves and to pursue those sexual practices as long as they are consensual. We have a right to be sexual even if it means that it results in an unintended pregnancy. We have a right to be sexual even if it means that we need an abortion.

There is risk to opening up and being vulnerable sexually with someone else, and with ourselves. And there is great potential for pleasure, intimacy, and closeness. So regardless of what happens in the process of being sexual, and regardless of whether there is an abortion, I will always affirm for individuals who come to the clinic and elsewhere that having pleasure and seeking pleasure are very important and worthwhile aspects of life to pursue. It is our right to make decisions all along the way that best meet our personal values for how to be.ABORTION may or may not be one of those decisions.

PART III

ORGANIZING FOR CHANGE: RELIGIOUS AND POLITICAL ACTIVISTS SPEAK OUT

OPTING OUT OF THE ABORTION WAR: FROM THE BIRMINGHAM BOMBING TO SEPTEMBER 11TH

MARGARET R. JOHNSTON

Author's Note: I wrote this piece in January 1998, right after the Birmingham clinic was bombed, killing a security guard and severely wounding a nurse. I was horrified by the assault and angry at the response of the media, anti-abortion activists, and even some of our pro-choice allies. I felt that the providers were taking the hits and yet the whole "war" scenario seemed to be working for everyone but providers. Even though I was trying to become less warlike, the piece still has an angry, confrontational feel to it, even after some edits. I decided to let it stand with only a few updates, and to write a postscript, to reflect what has happened to me "postwar." An additional note on "Lessons Learned from Terrorism" ends this account of my journey as an abortion provider.

1998

The television cameras pan the burned-out clinic, move in for a close-up of the ambulance, the shrouded body, the police looking grim, the clinic people comforting each other. The coverage of the 1998 Birmingham bombing of an abortion clinic is disturbingly familiar. "The latest casualty in the abortion war," intones a commentator, and then a representative of each side gets interviewed, "Grief, outrage, blah, blah, blah," and "We're not responsible, but abortion is violence, blah, blah, blah." We all know the drill.

In the pro-choice movement we have been lulled into accepting the idea that clinics are on the front lines of a war. Certainly it feels that way:

seven deaths, seventeen attempted murders, 206 acts of bombing or arson, 82 attempted bombings or arsons, 352 death threats, 682 blockades, 654 anthrax threats, 12,575 other acts of harassment, stalking, vandalism, etc.[12] Danger—from a piece of mail, a suspicious-looking person, and even a flower box as in the Birmingham bombing, is always possible. Vigilance is second nature to us; paranoia, a frequent companion.

But let's take a look at the metaphor and the reality of the Abortion War. There are "holy wars" elsewhere in the modern world. Northern Ireland, the former Yugoslavia, or the Israeli/Palestinian conflict. One side bombs a cafe, the other side kills someone in jail. A few mortar rounds destroy a temple, a few women get raped. Seventeen killed, a preemptive strike wipes out a pocket of enemy soldiers. That's war as we know it today.

So, what are the casualties—murders and attempted murders, on the anti-abortion side? *Zero.* How many crisis pregnancy centers have been bombed? *None.* How many blockades, stalkings, incidents of vandalism of right-to-life organizations? *Zip.* Even the number of "pranks" and harassment perpetuated against the anti's is infinitesimal in comparison.

Either the pro-choice side of the war is extraordinarily inept or this isn't a war. The sheer numbers tell a story of real violence and menacing behavior against abortion clinics and the people who work in them. This is clearly one-sided violence, or to name it—terrorism. You would think that there would be an outpouring of compassion and support for such embattled people, but I believe the American people cannot distinguish the victims from the combatants in the Abortion War. It's like the uninformed American perception of the Rwandan conflict: we don't see any difference between the Hutus and the Tutsis. They both seem awful and we don't care all that much if they continue to kill each other. It's a remote conflict between sworn enemies, whose positions we cannot begin to fathom.

If the American people can't get a good grasp of the issue and they want to tune out the Abortion War, they will see both sides as warlike. Hence, the expression, "extremists on both sides," which is nonsensical. This would explain the massive indifference to the very real casualties of this terrorist campaign: abortion providers. In the case of abortion, it's an unintelligible war for a lot of people, and it plays out along very simplistic notions about "innocent babies" and women having the freedom to have sex.

The polls are telling us that people see the anti-abortion activists as holding a deeply moral position which inspires them to extreme actions. They see pro-choice people as less extreme but also less moral. I would argue that when the pro-choice movement uses belligerent bravado, we weaken our case to an ambivalent American people. Yet, the pro-choice side persists in using war imagery; war rhetoric is rampant on both sides. Our language is completely battle-bound.

So, we must ask, who is perpetuating this war imagery? Who benefits from it?

Anti-Abortion Movement Embraces Violence

Well, first and foremost, the anti-abortion activists perpetuate and benefit from the War. In 1987 Randall Terry, founder of Operation Rescue wrote, "If you believe abortion is murder, act like it's murder." He, and Joe Scheidler, Keith Tucci, John Burt, and others transformed the meek, passive presence of older, largely Catholic women into a dynamic mobilization of angry men (and some women) eager to put their zeal into action. Their inflammatory and violent rhetoric was a clarion call to every violence-prone fanatic in the country.

The blockade era of the anti-abortion campaign led by Operation Rescue, for all its talk of "passive resistance" and "a peaceful presence" was, in reality, pretty rough. There was a lot of pushing and shoving and demonizing and deliberate risk-taking. Remember this? Clinics blockaded by a dozen or more protesters held "captive" by kryptonite locks and concrete blocks welded to cars—with full gas tanks. In town after town, the "Victim Lambs of Christ," led by Father Norman Weslin, created mayhem designed to make themselves look like victims, and the clinics, their protectors, and the police, look like the Gestapo.

But this phase of the movement created the righteous martyrdom necessary to escalate the terrorism. After being dragged across the pavement a few times, the activists got over the idea that breaking the law was a bad thing ("Higher Laws" and all that). They began to really see themselves as "victims," like the "innocent babies they were rescuing." (The Army of God manual is filled with such identity confusion: "We are just doing what the babies would do if they could protect themselves.") The anti-choice movement glorifies its martyrs and their sacrifices, and uses every rhetorical trick to justify escalating the risk, danger, and violence.

This new, emerging profile of an anti-abortion activist attracted violent, muddle-headed misfits who wanted to commit an act of "heroism" for a good cause. Michael Griffin, John Salvi, Paul Hill (all murderers of abortion providers) have made the news, but let's not forget Daniel Ware, picked up on his way to a memorial for Dr. David Gunn with a cache of guns. Or Michael Bray, convicted of conspiracy in a series of five or six bombings. Or Shelly Shannon, in jail for arsons and the attempted murder of Dr. George Tiller. Or Marjorie Reed, who was convicted of arson and spent some time behind bars. Or Eric Robert Rudolph, the missing suspect in the Birmingham bombing and the subject of a massive manhunt, now presumed dead.

The anti-abortion movement has done almost nothing to put the brakes on this violence. In fact, some are out-and-out gleeful, and call for more murders and bombings and busily researching good targets. Rev. David Troesch and fellow signers of the "Defensive Action" statement, put forward the "justifiable homicide" thesis on talk shows, and other venues including the Internet. "The Nuremburg Files," as well as other internet sites give names and identifying information for many who work at clinics or who are pro-choice. "Wanted posters" were widely circulated for Dr. David Gunn and Dr. Bayard Britton, both shot down by anti-abortion activists.

The violence has not tarnished the legislative and political successes of anti-abortion people, regardless of their willingness to be personally violent. Why is that? The Catholic Church has notably been silent in any attempt to de-escalate the violence. Anti-abortion Republicans have made no attempt to look into the campaign of terror that taints their cause. In fact, Ronald Reagan tacitly condoned the violence when it first erupted and right wing violence has escalated ever since.

In the absence of convincing denunciations of violence we can only assume that the anti-abortion spokespeople are like the Sinn Fein to the Irish Republican Army—different wings with exactly the same agenda and values. Certainly the rhetoric of the anti-abortion movement, from Senator to assassin, justifies the use of violence against abortion providers.

The Media Sets the Message

Who's next in line of the beneficiaries of war? In dollar sales alone, I think we would have to give this one to the media industry. Violence and sex are the mainstays of commercial journalism and the media is insatiable. A war right under their noses, especially one with undercurrents of sex and secrecy (i.e. abortion) is a boon to journalists. But even a good story is good only once. The anti's quickly grasped the necessity to escalate if they wanted to keep in the public eye. In the Birmingham bombing, the media pounced on this line: "There have been many bombings of abortion clinics, but this is the first fatality in an abortion clinic bombing." This statement normalizes clinic bombings and in a perverse way, encourages the escalation to murder with its attention. When Dr. Barnett Slepian was shot, it was billed as the "first abortion provider to be killed in his home." What will it take next to be the "big story?"

The nature of news today is that it is conflict driven and any other message is simply not heard. Any crossover of message is so confusing to the format that it is not tolerated. Unless, of course, there is a defector like Norma McCorvey, the original plaintiff in Roe v. Wade, now in the arms of the anti's. But then, there's another conflict and the media sells the war one more time.

Is Pro-Choice Pro-Provider?

There's another, on the face of it, unlikely beneficiary of the Abortion War, and that's the national pro-choice organizations. Groups like NARAL (National Abortion and Reproductive Rights Action League), Planned Parenthood Federation of America, and the Fund for the Feminist Majority are reliable counterbalances to the anti-abortion side and are professionally always available to comment for the pro-choice side. Within three hours of the bombing in Birmingham, Kate Michelman of NARAL had organized a press conference. Pro-choice organizations recognize all too well that the Abortion War is a great fund-raiser.

When the anti-abortion "troops" were at their most active in the late eighties, clinics suffered mightily. Patients chose clinics based on the picketer quotient. Leases were lost, vendors refused to come to clinics, and vandalism was at an all time high. Clinics under siege for long periods of time in Atlanta, Buffalo, and Wichita, for instance, took big economic hits. Pro-choice supporters opened their pocketbooks to all those who sent out an appeal about clinic violence. However, until fairly recently, when the Fund for the Feminist Majority made clinic assistance a priority, very few pro-choice resources translated into help for the clinics.

This is not merely sour grapes about money. While the anti-abortion activists targeted what they saw as the "weakest link"—the doctors—the pro-choice movement was still doing a rear guard action on restrictive legislation. But without providers, the possibility of choice for many American women was shrinking. From a strategy point of view, the pro-choice movement was locked into a rights-based strategy, ignoring the emotional appeal of the anti-abortion rhetoric. The bridge to a more effective message is real women's stories, a fact that providers have known all along. But many providers have been alienated from the pro-choice strategy, getting neither help with increased danger, nor interest in a different message.

With such high stakes it also becomes important to try to control the pro-choice response. During the blockade phase of the anti-abortion war, clinics were told to tell the media, "All scheduled patients were seen; no one was turned away" when that was clearly not the case. Clinics suffered terribly, many of them losing leases, patients, and going out of business. For clinics where the anti-abortion effort was prolonged, like Atlanta or Buffalo, the economic fallout was severe. But, the fund-raising biz was booming, and if the clinics suffered, no one knew it.

The pro-choice movement has made an investment in the Abortion War. This is not just a fund-raising tactic. Keeping up with the rhetoric of war affects legislative strategy, public policy debates, and most importantly, the public perception of how it is possible to think about abortion. The action/reaction stance of abortion rights activists narrowly defines acceptable cultural messages about abortion. Consequently, a rich contextual picture of the abortion experience is not available to us, or to women seeking abortion services. Women, and their partners and families, are still struggling with ill-fitting images of abortion as illegal, dangerous, and shameful. They have no cultural expression for feeling sad, disappointed, or for trying to do the right thing, much less for feeling empowered.

Abortion providers have taken the brunt of terrorism and have also been locked into keeping up with the war rhetoric. To change this is nearly impossible, even if you feel, as I do, that the strategy dooms us to more and more violence. In retrospect, providers have to acknowledge that we were willing participants in this collective bullet-biting. As providers under siege we hid our pain, like the child beaten up by the class bully. We didn't want "to give them anything," afraid that if we blinked in the stand-off we would lose our grip on legal abortion. But, more than a decade later, we still have a stiff upper lip and there are fewer of us. Legal abortion is no more or less secure, but we are definitely less secure. It's time to look at this turn-the-other-cheek strategy.

Abortion Providers: Are We Participating in Our Own Victimization?

My own group (providers) naturally concerns me the most. What do abortion providers have to gain by participating in a war where we are sitting ducks? As a group, our folks probably have more than our share of compulsive "helpers," risk-takers, and political warriors. You could also say that the mantel of martyrdom might fit some of us. This protracted struggle, peppered with danger and violence, certainly is satisfying to those personality types.

But more than anything, our rhetorical resistance to the terrorism directed against us protects us from feeling like victims. Angry words, militant posturing, and *de rigeur* battlefield bravery obscure the fact that we are powerless and largely defenseless against unseen terrorists. And let's face it: no one wants to be a victim. But if you are one, the next best thing is to put a brave face on it. So when the clinic in Birmingham displays signs that defiantly proclaim "this clinic stays open" and the owner reports that all staff came back to work, we have to consciously remember the cost of this courage.

When providers and clinic workers are viewed as superheroes we are not seen as human, and the public is once again encouraged to distance themselves from us. Our courage, however noble, does not speak to our good work, to *our* moral belief in what is at stake. Our brave but belligerent words do not articulate our dedication to giving women control of the choices in their lives. Our willingness to risk being targets shields the essential fact that women are the moral agents, making choices to better their lives. Besides, is it logical to have such an important right rest on someone's bravery?

Most providers feel that they do good, honorable, and valuable work. Years of vilification and silencing by the pro-choice movement, and living in fear of violence has left providers on the defensive. But, there are signs of change.

Some providers feel that acknowledging fear and vulnerability allows them to be open enough to continue to do their work. Some providers have found that the same strategies used in facing down screaming protesters have not served patients very well and they have switched gears. Personally, I have made a decision to disengage with the protesters as much as possible so that I can engage with my patients. Deborah Walsh (Charlotte, NC), who once carried patients on her back over a human barricade of anti's, reports that the Birmingham bombing tempted her "warrior side." "But I keep telling myself," she says, "my love is greater than their hate."[13]

"I'm tired of being on the defensive," says Renee Chelian, a Detroit provider. "We fought our battles, yet through it all we have been able to create an environment that allows women to see the changes they go through as normal and positive."[14]

Normalizing abortion is the anti's worst nightmare, and according to the Alan Guttmacher Institute, it is already happening. Forty-three percent of North American women will have an abortion by age 45.[15] Given that the Abortion War is not succeeding in real terms of stopping abortion, the strategy has become one of terrorizing providers and shaming women about their choice. While standing up for "unborn life," the anti's have condoned all kinds of violence, destruction, and murder. Their movement has never been on shakier moral ground.

It is time for providers, and pro-choice allies, to stand firmly on the high moral ground where millions of women make good choices for their lives. As providers, we know how our patients struggle to come to their decisions. As pro-choice people, we must not turn our backs on women's wisdom. The reality of our caring service must not be obscured by war whoops and undifferentiated antagonists in the Abortion War. We must resign our commissions as combatants and focus on our work. Listening to our patients, serving their needs, and providing good, sensitive medical care will, ultimately, be our best shield against violence.

We must shun the stigma of illegal abortion, speak out on our own behalf, and step off the battleground of the Abortion War. Let the public see us accurately—as victims of terrorism, but also as moral people dedicated to their work. Let us show the full picture of what we feel, not just the bravery, but the fear and grief. Let us allow ourselves to be human in the midst of a guerrilla campaign against us.

When we step off the battleground, the real combatants will be left: extremists and terrorists filled with hate and violence. They will not be seen as holy warriors defending the unborn if we do not respond with a rhetoric of belligerence, hate, and ridicule for those who are uncomfortable with abortion.

Where Are the Women?

When the smoke has cleared from the battlefield everyone can see what has been hidden: the women. The anti-abortion camp will have to face the fact that women, even their own women, have the power and the responsibility to say "yes" or "no" to life. And, no matter what the anti's do, women have continued to make those decisions in great numbers. The pro-choice side will have to admit their ambivalence about the reality of abortion. They will have to forego clean sound bites for the sometimes messy reality of women's sadness, repeat abortions, late abortions, the fallibility of birth control, and the "irresponsibility" of women as contraceptive users. Perhaps in looking at the diversity of women's choices, there can be the kind of peace that truth often brings. Might it be too much to imagine that the acceptance of many versions of morality will undermine the support that the radical Right fringe enjoys?

Regardless, I don't want to be part of this war any longer. I want to connect with the women that I see in full empathy for the complexity of their choices. And if some nut wants to take me out, I can't stop that. But no longer will I encourage the war by pretending I am "fighting" for "my side." My side is by the women who are making choices for their lives. The anti-abortion terrorists, and their more respectable supporters, will not be able to use me to justify their existence.

I don't fully know what the "battleground" will look like if we step off it. I don't pretend to be a pacifist who turns the other cheek, or who invites violence in civil disobedience. I have had my share of showdowns with Randy Terry and Joe Scheidler. I know I am an unlikely messenger of peace.

Yet, I am frustrated with the media that speaks of "extremists on both sides," with the anti's whose escalating violence goes on unrepentant, and with those "friends" who are invested in this war. And ultimately, also with the American public, fully half of whom have been touched by an experience of abortion, and who seem not to care.

I know, in my heart, that we are helping women who have made their own decisions. I trust them with their lives. My work is honorable and I want that truth to be seen. And, I am finding that I cannot speak this truth with warlike words and actions. But I am hopeful that our truths *will* reveal the reality obscured by the "War." And when it does, I want to be the one with an open heart, not the one with a gun.

1999-2000
PostScript: "It Isn't About Abortion!"

In the year and a half since writing this, I have taken some personal steps off the Abortion Battleground and have encouraged some of my colleagues to do the same. It hasn't been easy deconstructing a cultural phenomenon while still in it. Reporters investigating the War do not want to hear about a paradigm shift. Pro-choice activists, tired themselves, resent an "opting out" strategy and see their efforts as more likely to fail without a show of unity. Clinic workers, some of whom are beleaguered by violence, feel unsupported.

Confrontations with "my" protesters have diminished into nothingness and I even endeavor to call them "pro-life," as they want to be called, as a gesture of respect for a differing view. Although the possibility of violence remains, my day-to-day worry about it is fading. But the biggest change of all is how I conceive of my work of providing abortions to women. It started with a fundamental shift about how women see abortion—they don't! "I never thought I would be here" is the most frequent refrain from most women considering abortion. It was a shock to me to understand that *it isn't about abortion*. When I was able to refocus, it became clear that the key question is: "Is this the right time for me to bring life into the world, through my body?" In answering this question, the real picture of people's lives emerges in rich detail with recurring themes: the necessary limits of material resources as well as emotional resilience, the uncertainty of relationships in the modern era, the huge responsibility of parenthood (frequently *single* parenthood), the struggle to respond to an unexpected pregnancy ethically, and above all, the nearly complete misunderstanding of the abortion experience and pregnancy decision-making by our culture.

Once in a while a woman seeking abortion reports her hyperawareness of the negative images of abortion on television, in print, and in the small talk of her associates. There are almost no cultural messages that resonate with her reality. Women and men involved in an abortion experience need to feel that the complex issues they work through are seen as important, moral, complex by the larger community.

Providers realize that many women are unsupported not only by loved ones but also by the culture. In this hostile climate filled with misinformation, hateful name-calling, and desperate bids for secrecy, many women have no idea how to go about deciding about a pregnancy. To fill this void, I, with colleagues in many fields, wrote "Pregnant? Need help? Pregnancy Options Workbook," a guide that frames the decision around being responsible for life.[16] It offers information, discussion, exercises on basic decision-making skills, an even-handed look at all three options, and some cross-cultural perspectives on pregnancy loss and abortion, as well as a discussion of fetal development and basic reproductive health. After battling "the anti's" all these years, it came as a revelation to me that abortion politics is only a peripheral annoyance to women who are trying to decide what's best for their lives. But only after getting "unbound" from the battle could I find a way to write something useful for people facing this decision.

I now believe that the answer lies not in the struggle to protect abortion rights but in the challenge to create an abortion experience that addresses the complexity, diversity, and sometimes difficulty of an abortion decision with love, kindness, and respect. Providers are in a unique position, if they can see it, to respond to women and their families in a new way. They can listen to women and men about what this decision means to them, and reflect back to them the responsibility and the morality of their position. They can acknowledge the harder emotions of loss and shame and guilt while empowering women to embrace the future that abortion gives them. What could be more gratifying?

Changing the conversation about abortion one person at a time is rewarding, but it is also slow work. Capturing this paradigm shift in the Pregnancy Options Workbook has extended some of this understanding to women all over the U.S. and Canada. My colleagues and I are also trying to influence the training of abortion counselors and other staff so that more women can find a dreaded abortion experience to be transformational and validating.

As heartening as this is, we have yet to make even a blip on the media consciousness of the nation. We need help. We need the understanding of pro-choice people to create a momentum for a way out of the Abortion War. Here are some random suggestions I can offer:

Acknowledge the ickies. Supporters of full reproductive choice do not have the privilege of sitting down every day with women who are making a decision about pregnancy the way abortion providers and family planning workers do. But they can get in touch with their own experience and their own feelings about it. Acknowledging a full range of feelings, including the hard parts (or the "ickies," as one provider friend calls them). These might include repeat abortions, "late" abortions as defined by each person, or sex selection abortions, among other tricky topics. Exploring, and ultimately embracing our own ambivalence, will deepen our commitment to choice, not weaken it. Acknowledging differences makes us truly understand what individual choice is all about.

Break through the silence. Another strategy for pro-choice people is to talk about abortion compassionately at home, at work, at school, and with your friends. Identify yourself as someone who understands the complexities of the situation a woman faces and still comes down on the side of the woman who must choose what is right for her life. Break through the denial about this issue ("I thought it would never happen to me."). Make some room for the people around you to feel better about their decisions and about themselves. Challenge the image of guilt and shame, and affirm the morality of being responsible for life, whether "unborn" or full grown.

Support Abortion Funds. Pro-choice activists might also ally themselves with women directly by supporting abortion funds for women who cannot afford abortions or access to them. (Only fifteen states, as of this writing, pay for abortions through Medicaid and many have costly barriers such as parental notice, judicial bypass for minors, and twenty-four-hour waiting periods for women, requiring two visits.) In many places women must travel far to get an abortion incurring transportation costs, childcare expense, and lost work for themselves and the person who came with them. Despite the obvious need, abortion funds are the last to receive pro-choice dollars.[17]

De-gender abortion. Let's de-gender abortion, and parenthood too. Men have typically been shut out of the decision and the experience and the politics. But in real life they are part of the equation and pretending otherwise only reduces the number of people who will stand up for women. And it participates in the myth that men don't have a role to play in being responsible for life.

Lose the war rhetoric. Finally, are there ways to de-escalate the Abortion War in our own lives? What rhetoric are we using? Are we belittling people who disagree with us? Are we making it harder for well-meaning "pro-life" people when they face a difficult decision about a pregnancy? Can we afford to be less hateful to the other side? If not, what is the payoff for our own entrenched attitude?

Create a DMZ (Demilitarized Zone). How is change possible? We have yet to make a dent in mainstream culture. But a "sea change" happens when a critical mass of people change how they think and act. Like the bumper sticker says: When the people lead, the leaders will follow. We can have an impact on the culture because we are part of it. A pregnancy decision or an abortion experience could happen to someone close to any one of us, and we can make a difference for that person. Any one of us can carve out a small DMZ from the war, and in so doing change the experience.[18]

The Abortion War is perpetuated every day. Women have yet to see their reality reflected in the culture. The American people are still tuning out the abortion issue and turning their backs on what they see as inauthenticity on both sides. I still believe that a change is possible on this issue, but until the *New York Times* notices, I'll be listening, talking, and loving a change into existence. I hope you'll be doing the same.

2001-2002
Living With Terrorism, Some Lessons Learned

The terrorism of September 11th, 2001 has shocked the nation deeply. In the months following, as most people were struggling to adjust, most providers I know were saying, "Hey, this feels familiar!" Of course, most Americans thought that this was our first brush with terrorism, forgetting all the Black churches burned, the gay folks beaten, the abortion clinics terrorized. The incredibly diabolical boldness was what got to me; that sociopathic quality is what I associate with terrorists, whether they are home-grown or imported. Their actions are about power, not about cause, or belief, or religion, or even economics.

Sociopaths are attracted to divisive conflicts *because* there is room for terrorist activity; people who are otherwise passionate about something do not usually take the next step to terrorism, even if they support someone else who embraces violence. Every terrorist draws energy from a conflict and from that side of the conflict that most encourages violence. It is this social context that yields the most promise for action, the most hope for peace.

It's what I call the "ants at the picnic" phenomena. In the abortion context, when our patients are using the same words as our enemies we cannot help but notice that we have left "crumbs" that we need to clean up, so as not to "feed" the conflict. Post-abortion grief, fetal development information, fetal tissue disposal, and the religious/spiritual needs of our patients are some examples of our crumbs that keep the ants fed. Where would the anti-abortion folks be if every woman plumbed the depths of her soul, with the support of partner, family, and community, to arrive at a place of unshakable resolution and peace? What if every woman knew the facts about how far along her pregnancy was and what that meant, had her spiritual and religious needs addressed, and understood how to best care for herself emotionally after a pregnancy decision?

Both "our" terrorists and the Al Qaeda terrorists have the support and tacit (or even explicit) support of ordinary people. Let's look at the context that supports such hideous violence. Osama Bin Laden, or whatever groups are behind the terrorism, obviously enjoy(s) a great deal of support from the people. Why is that? What is feeding this conflict? And why don't Americans know anything about what goes on in the world?

We would be wrong to hear only the war whoops and miss the cries of injustice. While we work every day to amass wealth we cannot forget that the poorest among us in this country are better off than most of the people in Afghanistan, Pakistan, Iraq and any number of countries rife with terrorism. The wealthiest of Americans are richer than many whole nations. That most Americans are completely unaware of this disparity surely is feeding this conflict.

America's cultural obsession with "becoming a millionaire" does not cause a terrorist to pilot a jetliner into the World Trade Center. But our ignorance of the world's problems does give energy and righteousness to those who hate us and makes terrorism possible. When we refuse to notice world hunger, when we cavalierly cut off family planning dollars, when we tolerate mass slaughter in various parts of the globe, we leave crumbs for the terrorist ants to feed on and in the process, make ourselves righteous targets.

We are now in the middle of a war to root out terrorism. If we do not also address the context that feeds terrorism we will be at war forever. Just as with the Abortion War, if we truly want peace we must get past the war imagery and pay attention to what is happening to real people. Slim chance that this country will get on board, but it's perhaps the only chance we have.

ABORTION AND POWER:
THE EFFECTS OF PATRIARCHY AND CLASS ON WOMEN'S REPRODUCTIVE OPTIONS

Shaianne Osterreich

Secretary of State Madeleine K. Albright has volunteered to be the lightning rod for criticism from abortion rights groups if President Clinton compromises with Congress on a deal to free nearly $1 billion the United States owes the United Nations....A senior administration official was quoted as saying that "as a woman secretary of state, [Albright] knows instinctively the concerns of women's groups, and she is prepared to take the heat."
New York Times, November 12, 1999

In the Fall of 1999, Christopher Smith, a Republican Member of the House of Representatives from New Jersey led a campaign to hold hostage the payment of dues to the United Nations in exchange for the elimination of all United States funding for international family planning organizations that provide information about or promote abortions. As a woman who calls herself pro-choice, Madeleine Albright, then Secretary of State, the highest ranking woman in United States political history, decided that coming from her, other women would understand if she gave permission to negotiate the deal. As it turned out, the funding was not entirely eliminated but reduced by $12.5 million, a significant reduction to programs already underfunded. Albright and others used their economic power over the millions of women in less developed countries, for the sake of political and economic gain. This should serve as a reminder of how the issue of abortion, domestically and internationally, is entirely about the lack of power and control that women have over their own lives.

This essay will address the role that class relations play in shaping the choices that are available to women, specifically as they relate to their reproductive freedom. The legacy of the back alley abortion lives on for women all over the globe: those American women who find themselves relying on Medicaid or inadequate health insurance; women in Asia and Africa who are at the mercy of western funded international agencies, and many, many more. These women have in common their desire to control their bodies yet they are all constrained. They are held back by their minimal ability to wield bargaining power over the household and governmental resources that could shroud them in safety and hope instead of pain, poverty, and even death.

Political and economic power globally is not so different from such power closer to home. Class relations exist in our own Midwestern towns and hip urban cities just as they exist internationally. A woman's menu of choices, the options that she sees in front of her, are shaped by her perceptions, by what is legal, by what she can afford, by what she is aware of. All of these things contribute to how her life ends up. Deliberately or not, power plays by Albright and others, shape this menu. The passage of a bill here or there actually affects the choices and therefore lives of women all over the world. The interconnections of patriarchy and class provide a sound base upon which to limit the choices of poor women all over the world.

The World Health Organization (WHO) estimates that seventy-five thousand women globally die every year from unsafe abortions; those are often performed by family members, the women themselves, or untrained health workers. Even if they survive, women who want but cannot obtain safe, legal, and affordable abortions but try anyway, often go on to suffer from infertility, chronic morbidity, or other permanent physical damage. Combine this with the painful history of the United States' women before the landmark Roe vs. Wade decision, and we have clear evidence that women want to be able to control what happens with their bodies, even at extreme personal risk.

In the political situation of November 1999, Albright's political heroism as a 'lightning rod' was intended to channel the frustration of abortion groups in the United States so as to prevent voter retaliation against either Hilary Rodham Clinton or Al Gore, both running for election in the following year. Arguing that the sacrifice was critical to national security, and that not compromising would threaten global leadership, political policy-makers actually affected the shape of other women's individual lives. This was possible because of the international class relations that force less developed countries to be happy with what the developed world gives them. As the poor in the United States, poor countries are not in a position to bargain with their benefactors. Don't look a gift horse in the mouth remember? True, the pro-choice political leadership, including Albright, Clinton, Gore, and others, had their hands tied by being asked to engage in such a political compromise in the first place. But as a line in the Dylan song, *What Good am I*, goes "who tied them and why, and where must [they] have been?" Wanting an abortion is complicated business. The very first step of such a medical procedure ought to be to discuss it with one's doctor. However, in this case a woman might not even be able to talk about it with her regular doctor. Further, if and when she talks about it with a medical professional, it is not like other medical procedures. Can you imagine, on your own, tracking down the appropriate legal procedures and information concerning how to go about getting a tumor removed? Being asked, 'Have you seen photographs of this procedure? Are you capable of making this decision on your own? I think we will ask your parents, your husband, your mother-in-law, if it's ok'?

Economic studies confirm that income, and therefore class, play a role in a woman's ability to have an abortion. The majority of women who get abortions pay in cash. For those women who even have health insurance many policies refuse to cover abortions. (Many plans also refuse to cover birth control or prenatal care.) Further, it is unrealistic to rely on Medicare to cover an abortion, since sixty percent of state Medicaid programs limit abortion coverage to life endangerment, rape, and incest. Worse, South Dakota and Mississippi refuse to cover abortions even in these cases.

To compound the problem, with so many new restrictions being put on, such as waiting periods, multi-clinic visits, mandatory information sessions, and parental consents, many women find themselves having to make more than one trip, which can cause hardship, if they decide to do it at all. (There are even seven states with parental consent laws that require both parents to agree—that means Mom's permission is not enough.) If you live in Alabama, for example, where ninety percent of the counties in the state have no abortion providers, the implicit costs of such a trip are quite large. These include work or school time lost in driving several hours back and forth, not only once but twice. This is assuming of course, that the woman has the car, permission to use the car, gas, and so on.

The reasons why women get abortions can be quite diverse. In my late teenage years in my prosperous New England hometown, with my mother's fully comprehensive family insurance policy, my first gynecologist asked me what I would do if I got pregnant. I hadn't thought about it. She said very frankly, "Your insurance covers abortion, and we could do it right here, if that's what you would want. Just so you know." And for the rest of my life, I have known that. Even as I moved away from home, I always knew that abortion was an option that was conceptually and financially available to me. I have known that if I were to get pregnant I wouldn't have to stop going to school; my graduate degree would never be threatened; my career and my dreams would not have to be sacrificed for the sake of a baby. But, I also knew that if I did get pregnant and chose to keep the baby, my family and I could afford it. My ability to have an abortion would allow me my future—it would allow me to, at the very least, postpone the traditional job of motherhood. I could transcend the gender role that had been assigned based on my being a woman. It was liberating to have the safety net available. After all, this is one of the major arguments the pro-choice side presents for the legality of abortion.

But so many women cannot relate to this kind of liberation. First, there are those who do not see abortion as an option. They may not know and/or not believe that it's something they have access to. And financially, maybe it is not. Non-hospital abortions can cost as much as five hundred dollars in cash. Together with the implicit costs mentioned above, so many women legitimately see it as being out of reach. Low-income women are reported to spend twice as much time getting the money together for an abortion as middle or upper income women. Further, almost half of women who have abortions after the fifteenth week were delayed by problems with raising money, and/or finding or getting a provider. According to the American Medical Association, women who delay or are deterred in having abortions are more likely to bear unwanted children, continue potentially unhealthy pregnancies, or undergo abortion procedures that would endanger their health, such as those performed by non-medical staff or those that are done late in the pregnancy. Further, many states have restrictions on how far into the pregnancy a woman can be before it is illegal to abort.

But beyond access, class can inform an abortion decision in another way. I never had to sacrifice my budding career as an academic for the sake of a baby, but there are so many other reasons why a woman would want an abortion. What about the woman who cannot imagine having another child because she can hardly feed the ones she has? The waitress in Cleveland with three kids already. What about the woman in Tanzania, with five little ones, who grows the food the family needs to eat? Or the woman in rural Brazil who knows the coffee crops she produces for cash are paying low prices this year? These women are responsible for the household. In order to maintain, not transcend, their roles as good mothers, these women know that another baby would not be good for the family. They are not concerned about the child hampering their future career. Class imposes itself on these women by limiting the resources they have available to them to fulfill their roles as mothers. But what can they do? In this case, their options, those choices that they have, are framed by what they see as available, and they have little power to influence that menu of choices. But they don't do nothing. History tells us bitterly that they attempt to gain control; they try to self-induce miscarriages; they go to the back alleys of the world. Again, if they could they would, and even if they can't, they try anyway.

To be empowered is to be able to shape your menu of choices. Not those that are just legal, but that you can actually choose. They must be available, they must be affordable, and you must believe that they are options. For people who are committed to making others better off, it is a struggle to articulate what true empowerment entails. Borrowing from economist Amatrya Sen, I would argue that empowerment for women stems from a widening of the set of actually available choices. Women who are constrained not only by patriarchal ideas about womanhood but by class, need attention paid to their specific constraints. Access to safe and affordable abortions, as well as other family-planning alternatives, should not be a bargaining chip in a conflict over global leadership. That it is, is merely a reminder of the fact that a woman's menu of choices is framed by those around her and that how she lives her life, is not, in many ways, up to her. With Western pro-choice allies like Secretary of State Albright helping to frame those choices, who needs enemies like House Representative Smith?

A RADICAL LANGUAGE OF CHOICE

Krista Jacob

Over the past few years, many of us in the pro-choice movement have become increasingly frustrated with how the abortion issue is depicted in the mainstream media.

Admittedly, the media provides coverage of the abortion issue, especially during elections and in the aftermath of terrorist acts committed against doctors and clinics. The problem, rather, is with *how* abortion is talked about. Take, for example, the 2000 presidential race between Al Gore and George W. Bush. In each debate, Al Gore expressed his pro-choice position, stating simply: "It's her body, it's her choice." On the one hand, this is certainly true and, is the reason why our movement is called "pro-choice." Yet, on the other hand, abortion is more complex than simply being a matter of choice. For many women there are emotional, physical, spiritual, and other layers to their experience that are rarely acknowledged in mainstream discussions of abortion. When public support for abortion rights is limited to simply reciting a bumper sticker slogan, our very cause is being undermined.

Consider, in contrast, the tactics employed by the anti-choice movement: They use their vast economic resources to create a rich (albeit misleading) language opposing choice. They coin clever slogans, run manipulative television commercials, litter roads and highways with anti-choice billboards, and harass women's health clinics, patients and the doctors who provide abortions. They use religion to shame women who are choosing abortion (Abortion is a sin, God will punish you), and they promote negative views about sex (If you're gonna have sex, there's a price to pay. If you don't want to get pregnant, then don't have sex). Consequently, abortion is cloaked in shame, and millions of women who have made this choice remain silent.

Furthermore, while the anti-choice movement silences women, ironically, they co-opt feminist discourse, saying such things as: "Abortion is violence against women" and "abortion kills girls." Several years ago when I was walking into a clinic where I worked, a protester mistakenly took me for a patient and said, "You might be aborting a girl. Don't do it! I know a family who can adopt her!" Her interpretation of feminism, I'm afraid, was as simplistic and uninformed as her understanding of adoption policies.

The anti-choice movement also uses feminist educational campaigns about breast cancer prevention and post traumatic stress syndrome to perpetuate untruths about abortion, such as abortion causes breast cancer and women will suffer from post traumatic stress syndrome, which they have cleverly renamed "post abortion stress syndrome."

To be sure, the success of their movement has driven the abortion discussion farther to the right, and forced pro-choice activists to act from a defensive position, rather than a pro-active one. Subsequently, in an attempt to keep our heads above water, we overwhelmingly focus our efforts on keeping abortion legal, which is certainly a noble cause, but it's a battle we are losing because abortion is becoming less and less accessible, especially for adolescents, low-income women, and rural women. In other words, access to safe abortion is being restricted for women with the fewest resources and greatest obstacles (financial, parental consent laws, and geographical barriers). Women of means can afford to leave the country, or miss work, or pay for the cost of childcare, travel, a hotel or whatever additional expenses result from restrictions.

Even with the majority of Americans identifying as pro-choice, the anti-choice movement has created a climate that is hostile to abortion rights. A direct result of this hostility is that many of us pro-choice activists don't want to talk publicly about women's experiences that don't fit neatly into the "my body, my choice" slogan. In order to protect reproductive freedom, we want to say, "Let's not talk about *that* publicly because we might compromise our right to choose."

But, it is true that there are women who are not necessarily making a "free" choice. They may be confined by various circumstances, such as financial or relationship issues. Regardless, these women experience a complex mix of feelings that are rarely acknowledged in mainstream discussions of abortion. They may even feel marginalized within the pro-choice movement itself.

For example, a woman I know who had an abortion because her welfare benefits were terminated, said to me, "I didn't know that it was okay to feel regret about my abortion; even though I am pro-choice, I didn't think my feelings were politically correct." Sadly, she had been looking to the mainstream media as her source of information about what it means to be pro-choice, rather than to individuals and direct service providers within the pro-choice movement itself.

While there are women who don't feel like their decision to have an abortion was truly a choice, there are many more women who derive empowerment and strength from their abortion experience. Since abortion is an existential experience, it can provide an opportunity for women to examine every facet of their lives. Many women view their choice as a loving and compassionate one, not selfish. I've seen women make important changes in their lives—from ending an abusive relationship to fulfilling personal and professional goals to reconnecting with a lost faith—as they use their abortion experience to reclaim their bodies and their lives.

As a movement and as a society, we need to cultivate a radical language of choice that reflects the continuum of the abortion experience. This honesty will strengthen our movement, and provide much needed support and validation to the millions of women who make this choice.

A version of this essay originally appeared in the *Minnesota Women's Press* and in *Sexing the Political: A journal of third wave feminists on sexuality*, located at www.sexingthepolitical.com.

POSSIBILITIES VERSUS BABIES

Amy Blumenshine

I began this essay while I was aborting my third pregnancy. The blood that might one day have flowed through a child was instead oozing out of me, leaving me feeling drained, tired, and sad. Drop by inexorable drop, the possibility of new life within me was flowing away. I had wanted a baby. My husband and I had been trying to conceive for months. Staying pregnant, however, was not within our control. My body was rejecting the new tissue. My experience, while considered an abortion by the medical community, was what is more commonly known as a miscarriage.

While disappointed, I was not too upset. I knew that over forty percent of pregnancies miscarry. I knew that generally, the miscarriage occurs because something is wrong with the pregnancy. Some describe it as the body "deciding" that it's not a good idea to continue the pregnancy. Perhaps something is wrong with the intrauterine environment, or the body is not ready because of ill health or lack of sustenance to support a pregnancy. Perhaps the pregnancy has gotten in the way of other body processes that are necessary for survival. Any of these circumstances may be the reason for a body-decided abortion.

Even as the woman's body sometimes "decides" that the pregnancy should not be continued, the woman herself is morally and physically capable of making the same decision. It is up to her to decide whether the environment, the family situation, and her resources—emotional, physical, and financial—can meet a baby's needs. Perhaps she feels unable to continue without the support of the prospective father. Perhaps the family environment is poisonous or hostile, and a child would be warped or mutilated psychologically. Perhaps the well-being of her other children would be jeopardized by expanding the family. The woman, like her body, can make the decision that it's not a good idea to continue the pregnancy.

The power of reproduction carries with it the burden of making significant decisions. While some long for a simpler world in which such choices are in divine hands, the reality is that a reproductive woman herself makes those important decisions on a day-to-day basis.

She decides whether to protect herself from involuntary insemination by undesirable partners. She chooses how to navigate safely through a world of toxins, including tobacco, alcohol, street drugs, lead, pesticides, industrial hazardous waste, and nuclear emissions. She chooses whether to get pre-natal care and how to care for herself while pregnant. Upon the birth of a child, she chooses whether and how she will care for the baby. Clearly, her alternatives vary according to her income and other resources, but if she makes bad choices resulting in child neglect or abuse, the legal system will treat her like a criminal. A woman has decisions to make, whether she likes it or not.

Some religions teach that choosing an abortion is the same as murdering a baby. From the moment of conception, they say, the fetus has a soul. Yet only since abortions have become an issue have those same religions treated miscarriages with any special respect. The body-discarded tissues resulting from spontaneous abortions were not previously offered baptisms or funerals. The moment when some tissue becomes sacramental is primarily a cultural and psychological determination.

Culturally, I weigh the welfare of children first. I am a softy about children because I am the tired but ecstatic mother of two little ones. I considered my two completed pregnancies and childbirths to be spiritual, as well as exhausting, nauseous, and emotionally challenging states.

Quite simply, I do not regard fetuses as babies—little people—I consider them as amazing possibilities. When I mourned my early miscarriage, I was not mourning for a real baby, but for that particular possibility of a baby. The miraculous combination of tissues growing in my body had the possibility of developing into a human being, but much could happen—and did—before that occurred. The sadness I felt at the time has been completely overshadowed by the intensity and joy of birthing two real babies.

There's no question that the DNA for a new human body existed in my miscarried fetus—as it does also in my other drops of blood. Now that we know about the role of DNA in determining life, our best understanding of life is as a continuum of possibilities for reproduction. Life in that sense never does "begin" because the essential code for life is ever present. The abortion was a sort of death, the death of that particular possibility of a human being, one of many such deaths that we are party to, not unlike the death of hope that some children of poverty experience.

Psychologically, what we feel about the situation has a lot to do with what we think. If we imagine fetuses as babies, we naturally feel protective towards them. Early in the pregnancy of my first child, I had trouble believing I was pregnant, but by the last trimester, I felt as though I was sharing my skin with another person! With my second child, I had many nauseous reminders of being in the early stages of pregnancy, but our significant bonded human relationship began later. I did feel that bond with my children in the last trimesters, but I still knew that I didn't have a baby until I successfully birthed one and could hold her in my arms.

Before I ever birthed a child, I did once choose an abortion. My husband and I were students in graduate school when I became very sick. I discovered that I was suffering both from the early stages of pregnancy and a uterine infection. If I had been forced to continue that pregnancy, I probably would have died, or, at best, lost the ability to have children. As it turned out, I began to miscarry, but the doctor still felt an abortion was necessary to flush out the infection. Thank goodness that all those medical decisions were not subject to legal red tape and potential criminal prosecution. Instead, health professionals could give me the speedy care that I needed.

The advocates of mandatory childbearing would like women to believe that they will be forever tormented by having chosen an abortion. In my case, I can still remember the flood of relief I felt after the procedure. It stands in my memory as a shining day of rising above being crushed by the fate of my biology. I could overcome being a mere vessel for an unwanted and unwise pregnancy.

And I wish that others had made that choice rather than setting up a life of abuse and neglect for their children. For I believe that every child deserves to be wanted. Lynn, a Minneapolis woman I know, has just found out that the child she gave up for adoption three years ago has been living in a series of foster homes all this time.

Another toddler, born to a teen mother at the same time as Lynn's baby, had to watch his mother's boyfriend stab her to death. These girls did not want and could not take care of babies, and society failed to take care of them as well. What medieval thinking encouraged their pregnancies to be carried to term? It would have been better for those children if those women had had the unequivocal choice about completing their accidental pregnancies.

It is a tragedy, yet a grim reality, that our society does not provide well for unwanted children. Accordingly, it is even more essential that each woman assert her right, to the best of her ability, to determine what happens to and through her body. Indeed, I consider women to be better ethical agents than the biological functioning of our bodies. I do not believe that women are making decisions reserved to God when we assume the awesome responsibility for the fruit of our wombs.

One argument for coerced pregnancy is that abortion removes from the human network needed and unique qualities of the individual who was the possible outcome of the pregnancy. The God that I believe in is not so easily thwarted!

If I were to experience an unplanned pregnancy in the future—for all birth control is fallible—I don't know what I would do. I am sure that I would have feelings about a possible baby, and that my decision would not be easy. I would have to weigh a lot of factors and consider the well-being of a lot of people in seeking the right choice. Increasingly, I fear that a bunch of men, who have never felt what women have felt, are stripping us of our ability to be responsible.

From my experience, complex moral reproductive responsibility best rests with the women most intimately involved. We do weep for those lost possibilities, but those possibilities are not the same as babies.

MY PRO-CHOICE CREDO

Kathleen George Kearney

On a very public level, this nation appears to relish abortion politics. Struggles have included the tragedy of a twelve-year-old impregnated through rape by her brother, a suspect in a deadly clinic bombing who continues to elude authorities, and Congressional attempts to limit the accessibility of abortion, including medical and late-term procedures. Within these stories there are those loud voices claiming that in order to be religious, one must be opposed to reproductive choice.

My belief in abortion as a moral, ethical, holy, and empowering choice comes from a variety of factors. My religious faith is one of those factors. In my work as an activist, counselor, and minister, I have seen firsthand how abortion can be the most faith-filled option in pregnancy, and that to be pro-choice is to affirm the strength of women and of religious faith.

I am part of the Minnesota Religious Coalition for Reproductive Choice, which represents various denominational groups and religious individuals, including those who are Catholic, Jewish, Methodist, Presbyterian, Unitarian, and of the United Church of Christ. We are religious people of diverse faiths who are united in believing that freedom of conscience is as essential as freedom of religion. I am only one religious voice among many. But at a time when much of the rhetoric about abortion includes misinformation and judgments, it is important to remember that religious people are also pro-choice people.

I am a product of the Presbyterian Church, raised to believe in a God who calls for the transformation of our communities and of our own selves. This transformation creates justice. The compassion of God is matched by the passion of God to continually push us into new lives as agents of change and healing. This moral agency extends to women who choose to terminate their pregnancies. I believe in a God who holds up pregnancy not as a punishment, but as a celebration when planned and wanted, and a tragedy when unplanned and unwanted.

The Jesus I know believed all people to be worthy of care and salvation. In the Bible, it is obvious that Jesus loved women. He listened to them, stayed in their homes, and discussed the kingdom with them. Jesus depended upon women disciples for financial and spiritual support. Just as Jesus was present with women throughout his ministry, Christ is present with those women who have abortions. Christ waits upon women, just as women waited upon him, as he preached love and justice, as he died for what he believed, as he rested for three days, and then rose from the dead.

It is not ironic that many women in the Bible remain anonymous. In public discourse, whenever we talk about abortion we mention politics, ethics, morality, theology and economics. Rarely do we acknowledge that at its core, and in the end, abortion is about one woman making a decision based on the reality of *her* life. In order to wisely and fairly discuss abortion, we must base our words on the experiences of women, and not on our own political or religious sensibilities.

The Bible condemns many things. Abortion is not one of them. The Bible has nothing to say about abortion. Many Scriptural directions for moral living are open to interpretation. Even the prophetic announcement that we must do justice, love kindness, and walk humbly, leaves one wondering what that means in practical application. The ambiguity and the freedom of Christianity can be frightening, overwhelming, exhausting, exciting, and deeply moving. One of the most fantastic things about God is God's mystery. Grace cannot be predicted or controlled; it breaks in when and where we are open to its infusion. Surely, women who face tough pregnancy decisions are open to (and often hoping for) such an infusion. The power of grace and the presence of God allow for a plurality of beliefs and personal truths. As the body of Christ, as whole people of God, we are called to act upon our beliefs, and to live out our own truths.

As the body of Christ, as whole people of God, we are called to act upon our beliefs and live out our truths as best we can, as lovingly as we can.

God weeps when we are hurt, and rejoices when we are made whole. I believe God stands with women as they end pregnancies, just as God stands with women who deliver babies and with women who give those babies to adoptive parents. God does not choose God's allegiances. God stands with all of us, regardless of where we stand. The challenge is to stand where we are with integrity, compassion, and wisdom. When women choose to have abortions, they are acting with integrity, aware of compassion, and in realization of their own wisdom. To doubt the integrity, compassion, or wisdom of women is to insult women and offend God. At times it is and will be difficult to support women in their experiences of pregnancy, but if we are to be faithful to God and Christ, we must stand beside women and support them in lives of their own choosing.

MIDLAND COALITION FOR CHOICE

Carole Head

It would be nice to be able to say that the world is catching on, that it is coming around to our way of thinking. But knowing that is a dream, here is what our small group of volunteers has been able to accomplish.

We are the Midland Coalition for Choice, a group of about a dozen women (mostly white-haired), with a mailing list of close to seven hundred. In 1989, Judy gathered together an informal group of women representing four local organizations. These were the League of Women Voters, the American Association of University Women, National Organization for Women (NOW), and Business and Professional Women. The latter group dropped out after about two years because of conflict over the abortion issue within its membership.

We have two simple objectives. The first is to educate people of both genders about what choice is, and the second, to provide funding for abortions when someone either has no funds or no one to fall back on for help. We certainly do not have unlimited funds, so we limit our assistance to first trimester cases (with rare exceptions), and will only provide financial assistance one time per person. We have also funded vasectomies at the request of the local health department. We have taught minors how to get a judicial bypass, which is requisite in Michigan for minors who cannot get parental consent. On the education side, we have held programs on Roe v. Wade anniversaries in which speakers share information—speakers like Alexander Sanger, and, another time, a woman Episcopal priest. We have held outdoor public rallies with speakers, too, but these are difficult to perpetuate since the anniversary date is in January. In February of 2001, we represented the "choice" side in a sixty minute PBS debate for our area. Using a local gynecologist, a minister, and Planned Parenthood's legislative director for Michigan, we got a lot of public exposure and won for the cause against representatives from Crisis Pregnancy, a nurse, and a representative of Right to Life.

We also interview local candidates running for a seat in the Michigan House of Representatives. People on our mailing list are then sent a current listing of pro-choice candidates (for that seat, as well as others on the ballot). We have been on radio roundtables and have written "Forum" pieces in our local newspaper. We have been the recipients of Planned Parenthood of East Central Michigan's Stewart R. Mott Leadership Award which carried a stipend of five hundred dollars. The money was given to our County Health Department for use in their family planning section. Finally, we have run many taped programs from Planned Parenthood on our local television station, MCTV.

The question we are asked most often is about money. How is it raised? Once a year we write a letter to our mailing list detailing what we have accomplished in the past year, and what issues we anticipate for the next year. At the bottom of the letter, we print a two-inch cut-off piece, which asks for contributions. Contributions from twenty-five dollars to two hundred and fifty dollars roll in. Many sign to give a second twenty-five dollars within the year, if it is needed. About one hundred and fifteen people are regular contributors to the Jane Doe fund. Over fifty others contribute to education or "as needed." Others need to be called. When we started the organization, we simply called people we knew and asked them for twenty-five dollars. At the same time, the founding organizations put the word out through their newsletters.

In the past, Sally[19] has acted as our liaison between the person needing help and the women's health clinics. Women would hear about our services by word of mouth, or be directed to us through a clinic, or, on the rare occasion, by a doctor. They'd get Sally's phone number. She would hear their story by phone and, if they met our requirements, she'd ask them to set up their date with the clinic and call her when they had it. Only then did she give them her address. She would call our treasurer who would get a money order with the clinic's name on it. Clients would go to her house to pick it up along with a discussion about condoms, safe sex, and so on, and then learn that they could not call on us again. They are always grateful for the help. They are asked to start paying us back when they get ahead. But the truth is, not one person has ever sent us a nickel.

Presently, we skip the money order part and send the check for our share directly to the clinic once the clinic tells us the date is confirmed. However, we still talk with the woman to make our points clear.

Stories

There was a fourteen-year-old who heard about us through a nurse. Examination found this child's pregnancy well into the second trimester. She had had a "one-night stand" with an out-of-town acquaintance. When she called him, he simply said, "Well, that's your problem. You girls should be more careful." Why didn't she come earlier? Because she was anemic and used to having irregular periods. Her mother refused to provide any assistance. However, she was told by the nurse about the judicial bypass option. She took herself down to the Probate Court. Here she met a court assistant who knew about the Coalition and helped her through the paperwork. The assistant also called us to be certain money would be available.

There was a twenty-four-year-old, single mother of two. This woman was under a doctor's care. She was provided birth control pills. These failed, and she had her first child. The prescription was changed and upgraded in strength, but that, too, failed and she had her second child. In desperation, she got the Depo Provera shot. When she went in for her second shot after three months, she found herself pregnant again. Here was a pregnancy due to contraceptive failure. Referred to us by a local clinic, she was desperate and we came to her rescue. This woman's plan is to save her money for a tubal ligation.

In a perfect world, we would not need to go through all of this. In a perfect world, abortion would not be needed, and no one would need our help either.

DIVERSITY IN CHOICE

Alice Limehouse

A misconception floating around in these turbulent times is that pro-choice equals pro-abortion. It is part of the way we all try to categorize everything into neat little boxes and often neglect the gray areas in our lives and in society. There are many people who are surprised at the idea that a Republican could be a feminist, or that a lesbian could be theologically conservative. Although I am not a Republican, theologically conservative, nor a lesbian, in my life I have come across many individuals who failed to fit into my categories. By virtue of being multifaceted human beings, they have, as I do, various, seemingly contradictory, characteristics living side-by-side in their personalities and life styles.

This brings me to my story. The summer leading up to and the fall semester of my senior year in college, were among the most fun and exciting times of my life. I was doing very well academically at my liberal women's college as a Religious Studies major. I was an assistant manager at a popular women's clothing boutique in a fashionable part of the city. I was nearing completion of the Discernment by Church phase of my process to ordination in the Episcopal Church, and had received positive and encouraging feedback. Two or three nights a week I was hitting the town, Latin dancing with my girlfriends. I was Salsa-ing my way through life and savoring every delicious bite. The spiritual self, the intellectual, and the lover of life were all passionately alive within me.

These high times carried me through the holidays. In February, I went to Boston and New York City to interview for admission to two of the most prestigious Episcopal seminaries in the world. Five weeks later, the same week I received my acceptance letter to my first choice school, I discovered that I was pregnant. Three months until college graduation, acceptance to seminary, and well on my way to ordination in the Episcopal Church, I was single and pregnant. My world seemed to deflate.

If I had been one of my friends or professors and was in the position of giving me advice, I would have brought up abortion. Not only my friends and professors, but my parents, brother, and ministers gingerly, lovingly suggested abortion. If anyone had asked me before I was pregnant what I would do if I were to become pregnant, my unhesitant answer would have been to have an abortion. But when I was really pregnant and I had to choose in real life, not in theory, I chose to carry and keep my baby.

When my time came to choose, I went with what my heart and soul were crying to me and chose to become a mother. The initial decision was as easy as turning on a light switch. Immediately thereafter, however, I found myself being questioned, from all sides. Why wouldn't I have an abortion? Didn't I realize that I was throwing my life away? Wasn't I a feminist? Didn't I believe in reproductive freedom? A particular person who was close to me made it clear that she thought I was betraying the cause by not exercising my right to an abortion. She felt that I was tossing all that I had gained through education and professional experience, as well as all that had been gained for me and all women through our history of feminism, out the window. I found myself questioning my motives, wondering if I was really doing the right thing.

Then I got angry. My decision was based on what was right for me, an educated, independently thinking, creative, spiritually centered woman. No one else, no matter what their causes or reasons, had any right to tell me I was wrong. This, my friends, is the very root of the pro-choice movement: It is the right to make our own choices with our own bodies, without explanation or justification. It was my choice.

I am now the single mother of a walking-already nine-month-old daughter. My pregnancy, our childbirth experience, and her little life have given me a new appreciation and awe for the life-giving creative process of which we are all, women and men, a part. Although we have been blessed with good health, the ride has not been all tea and roses. There is a lot of prejudice in our society against single parents. This is especially true of single mothers who are often perceived as statistics, while single fathers are perceived as heroes. It has been very difficult financially. Right now I cannot afford to live in an apartment and must live with my parents, a real blow to my pride and independence. The hardest consequence of my choice was that I was forced to give up my aspirations to the ordained ministry. I had worked very hard, both academically and in the church mandated process, and had completed everything except seminary. My faith in God has not faltered, but my ideas about church have.

My life is a portrait of a pro-choice woman who chose to not have an abortion. To many, this may seem a contradiction in values. I may be perceived as one who missed the point. I may not fit neatly into one of the category boxes. This is all right by me. I have learned through my experiences to dismantle the categories and to honor the gray areas. I have learned the true value of the freedom to choose.

ABORTION IS A CONSTITUTIONAL RIGHT

Jennifer Olencheck
President, Milwaukee National Organization for Women

"Roe gave the right to choose abortion the same fundamental constitutional protection as the right to vote...Under Roe, a state law favoring one childbearing choice over another is just as unconstitutional as a law favoring one political party over another."[20]

The right to choose abortion is a constitutional right. This is the only health care service debated in the church, in the legislature, in the media, at the clinics, in the courts, and on the streets. I can't realistically imagine having any other constitutional right and its merits debated daily. For example, is the right to vote a personal choice or should there be restrictions? What if you were only allowed to vote if you were a victim of rape or incest, or lived in a big city, or could afford to travel to another state to vote? This is ridiculous, of course. So, why aren't the same types of protections that are guaranteed with our right to vote, also guaranteed to women and their right to choose abortion?

The tremendous victory on behalf of women's lives, women's choices, and women's autonomy that Roe gave us was short-lived. From the very moment Roe was decided, anti-choice proponents have been trying to take this constitutional right away from women. Only through Roe is an independent, capable woman's ability to choose on her own behalf questioned. "If only she had more time to think about her decision, I know she would change her mind" is an argument anti-choice forces use to support waiting periods for medical procedures. "Women are not possibly capable of making such a momentous decision on their own" is the argument anti's use to impose laws allowing states to force women to sit through state-scripted, anti-choice lectures, in addition to the countless other restrictions placed on legalized abortion today. Can you imagine going to the polls to vote and being forced to hear an anti-candidate lecture and then wait twenty-four hours before being allowed to vote? If only you heard what the other candidate(s) has to say, you would surely change your mind, right?

This would never be allowed to happen because the right to vote is a personal right protected by the United States Constitution. But the right to choose abortion is also a personal right protected by the U.S. Constitution. Why, then, are restrictions and clinic harassment allowed to occur? Why are women's choices and their ability to make those choices made into a public issue? Why are women forced to privately pay for a right guaranteed to every woman in America—you don't have to pay to vote do you? It is absurd that these things can, and do, happen to a freedom protected by our Constitution.

We must continue to fight for total reproductive freedom and for a constitutional amendment that says women are equal and capable participants in society. You can make a difference: speak up when you hear people talking negatively about women who have abortions; volunteer with your local NOW (National Organization for Women) chapter, other pro-choice organizations, or at a women's health clinic; share your knowledge and opinions on why abortion must be safe, legal, and accessible (don't feel as if you shouldn't impose your views on others—the anti's do it all the time); tell your story if you've had an abortion, and make your elected officials hear your voice.

Choosing abortion is never an easy decision, but women make, and have been making, this decision for thousands of years. If Roe v. Wade were overturned, we would see thousands of women dying each year due to back-alley botched abortions. Contrary to popular belief, the legalization of safe abortion procedures does not increase the abortion rate, but does allow women to utilize safe and legal medical services. The right of women to choose whether to have an abortion is essential in exercising the basic right to control their own bodies.

The focus in the abortion debate should be on women's lives—women dying from back alley abortions, and women and doctors being threatened daily at clinic doors. Abortion must remain legal or women will die. We should remember Justice Harry Blackmun and be thankful that he had the courage to stand up and protect the right of women to control their own bodies. His choice has saved the lives of thousands of women.

FREEDOM OF RELIGION

Reverend Marguerite A. Beissert

I was the first clergy counselor in the New Jersey Clergy Association for Abortion Counseling (pre-1973). In 1992, I received a Freedom of Religion award from the Religious Coalition for Abortion Rights of Southern California.

I was ordained in 1971 in Summit, New Jersey, on a Sunday afternoon. Monday morning, the pastor I was associated with drove me to a meeting of the New Jersey Clergy Association for Abortion Counseling (with my whole-hearted consent!). As I walked into an "army" of men, I was the lone woman there. When I was introduced, the applause was hearty.

I realized later that these men had been counseling women on an innately feminine concern. I understood my reception. Then I began counseling women on this subject, but also began to get involved in something I had not counted on: debates. I was asked to participate in organized presentations that often felt more like bitter attacks.

Prior to my participation in the association, I had been giving an address in Puerto Rico where abortions were available to counselees. Now I also had a New York clinic address.

I did not enter this kind of counseling without some theological digging. I felt then—and still do—that when the Hebrew Testament declared that God gives us dominion over the earth, this is passing on to us *responsibility*, which means the freedom and the duty to make decisions, always, of course thoughtfully and prayerfully. In addition, as a person who was emerging in my own right as a woman in a field very sparsely populated with female clergy, I recognized our need as women to have "dominion" or "responsibility" for our own decisions, especially about our own bodies.

If I had had any doubts, they have been dispelled by the people I have counseled. Here are two examples:

A man and his wife, who had taken three buses to reach me. The man's work was seasonal. They were Roman Catholic and had eight children, and she was pregnant. Do I need to say anything about offering an adequate quality of life to a newborn child?

An adolescent girl, smacking gum, with four boys waiting in another room for her. As we talked, it became abundantly clear that she was exhibiting defiance against her father's strict discipline. Still making gum bubbles, she said "I don't think I'm ready to be a mother." I strongly agreed.

I was careful in counseling these people. I told them I did not know if I would have the courage to decide in favor of abortion for myself. However, I am in a good marriage with a supportive husband. While an unplanned child may have stressed the family budget, we could have made it. My situation was not the desperate situations I was hearing about.

Occasionally, even in retirement, I still hear from those who seem to feel suicide is the only solution. We talk. I am not pro-abortion, as anti-abortionists want to label us. I am pro-choice. My hope is that decisions about child bearing be made within a family, by both husband and wife (or partner), but I strongly believe the final option belongs to the woman. It is her body and her life.

Excerpted from:

WOMEN AS WOMBS, WOMEN AS HOLES:

ABORTION, PROSTITUTION, AND THE SEXUAL EXPLOITATIONOF WOMEN

Chris Stark

In male supremacist lexicon there are two basic kinds of women: breeders and whores. The breeder women (wives) may double as unpaid domestic laborers, trophy wives, or they may even earn a second albeit smaller income. But under male supremacy wives exist primarily to pass along the man's genetics and name to the next generation, thus insuring his immortality, inheritance line, and next-to-godliness if not God himself. Under male supremacy, whores are both the outcasts of womanhood, those destined not to bear children or clean house, and they are the defining meaning of the female sex. Whores exist to be fucked. Period. They do not have children or families or meaning in life beyond the fuck.

The Christian patriarchs hated women, women's bodies, and therefore sex so much that they changed their mythology from one which spoke of Jesus (God's only son) as having been born from Mary and Joseph's copulation to one in which Jesus was born minus the earthly sin of sex.[21] In the Old Testament and in parts of the New Testament, Jesus not only had an earthly father and mother, but brothers and sisters as well. Jesus' brothers and sisters changed over the years into stepbrothers and stepsisters, then into cousins when the Christian patriarchs decided that both Mary and Joseph needed to be virginal. After the Christian patriarchs turned Mary into a virgin they wrote in the New Testament, "a midwife declared that

Mary's hymen remained undamaged during the birth of Jesus."[22] The Virgin Birth became a story about Mary's personal chastity, ethereal impregnation, and biological intactness. The proof were the words of a midwife and the physical exam someone (supposedly) performed on a woman, opening, holding open, probing, feeling for that piece of intact tissue. The Mother of God was examined like a cow, fingers inserted into her vagina to determine her sexual status: Virgin Queen.

In the Bible, a lie (the virgin birth) categorized women into the mother/whore complex. At the heart of present day misogyny lies the belief that Original Sin is sex, sex and sin are female, a baby is gestated in and born out of the female, it is delivered out of the tunnel in which the sin of sex is committed. Therefore the baby is born contaminated, dirty, and sinful. The sin-laden infant must be cleansed by a man with magical (holy) water. Jesus had to be born and die for humankind because, as infants, humans are born dirty and sinful. But to be more precise, because sex and birth are contaminated by contact with the female, sin is ultimately female. Therefore, the root of sin is female. In Christian mythology, Jesus really died for the sins of the women, their physical uncleanness, their dirt, their filth, their cunts, their monthly blood, their holes leading to the great void—that metaphysical mystery men have striven to understand through literature, art, politics, science, and religion.

Since women (mothers and whores) are the cause of sin, they are blamed and stigmatized for just about everything under the sun. This includes abortion, rape, rapists, unwanted pregnancies, prostitution, pornography, sexual desire, wife beating, unhappy childhoods, serial murderers, incest, and even the sexual abuses committed by former president Bill Clinton.[23] In all actuality, men have come to realize, in the most literal sense, that it would be better to pull the baby directly out of the womb, avoid the birth tunnel and in the process dig out the sin, mutilate the womb, the woman herself. If the early Christian patriarchs had possessed the foresight to see contemporary technology they probably would have had Jesus born of a petri dish, thereby further evading the contamination of a woman's body. If men could find a way to create babies without women, they would. When they do, they will. Then, of course, there will only be the need to create baby future men (boys), except for the occasional baby girl who will serve as a fuckstation whore for the daily gang bangs when the men grow tired of using blow-up dolls, womb machines, and plastic vaginas.[24]

As sex is sin is dirt is filth to the contemporary Christian patriarchs so it is to the present day liberal pornographers. The Christian patriarchs and the pornographers are friendly enemies. They may fight on a radio call-in show about whether the U.S. women's soccer team was pornographic when they pulled off their shirts after the winning goal, but they have much more in common than not. Christian and non-Christian men alike prostitute women and girls, buy women and girls, use pornography, beat and kill their wives and girlfriends, and rape their wives and daughters in the home. Men hate women. They are terrorists in their hatred of women, assassinating women and girls and every so often an abortion doctor. They put hit lists out on women and abortion doctors.[25] Men control women's sexuality and reproduction and the ability of women to terminate or carry out their pregnancies. They punish women for being women. They are men. It follows then, that it does not matter what women do, whether they are good girls or bad girls, wives or whores, black or white, ugly or pretty, tall or short, left-handed or right-handed, they are bitches (holes) and they must be punished.

The oppression of women begins in the body, in men's visceral hatred of the female body. Subsequently, women live in and as colonized bodies. Women will never be emancipated until they unequivocally control their bodies. Period. As it is now, women do not control their bodies, not in sex or in the reproductive aftermath of sex. Reproduction cannot occur without intercourse (unless through a rare occurrence of parthenogenesis) or the sexual medical intervention of scientists and doctors. Abortion rights cannot be separated from the rest of women's rights, like a limb amputated and left to stand on its own, the fight for abortion rights is destined to fail, dissolve into the never-never land of liberalism, unless it is connected to the rest of the body of women's rights. Given that women do not control sex they cannot control abortion. Sex, abortion, reproduction, housing, livable wages, nutritionally adequate food, education, affordable daycare, freedom from racism, classism, and heterosexism, and freedom from prostitution and pornography must be realities in all women's lives before women can have rights other than the so-called natural rights historically assigned to them.

If men got pregnant abortion would be a sacrament.—Pro-choice slogan

This pro-choice slogan is clever, but inaccurate because women would not be women, socially, politically, legally, or culturally if they did not bear children and therefore need abortions. Men do not need abortions. The dominant sex class does not ever need to get an abortion, no matter how many times the individual man has fucked or made love or raped, he never needs to worry about becoming pregnant. It is not his problem. So, if men got pregnant, abortion would be illegal or legal in name only and unavailable to most men (especially men-of-color) because if men got pregnant they would be women, they would be the subordinate sex class, they would be oppressed, subjugated, discriminated against, downtrodden, raped, and beaten in droves. They would be sold into prostitution. Their bodies would be objectified, dehumanized, tortured, photographed, and sold as entertainment for the other sex. They would be medically experimented upon under the aegis of reproductive technologies when they or their wives were infertile. In short, in a hierarchical sex class system, it would not be possible for men to bear children and still retain the rights of the privileged sex class. There would be no holy man in robes sanctifying abortion. There would be no legal system enforcing the holiness (availability) of abortion. It is women's bodies, their gross anatomical differences as compared to the defining human (male) which positions them as the subordinate sex. The ability to bear children is the basic physical difference between men and women. This sexual difference, or sexual abnormality, is used as an excuse to keep women in the home, having babies, segregated and paid less in the workplace, raped, and generally hated.[26]

Motherhood has traditionally been the political institution that defines what it means to be a woman. Mother is the individual unit; her life is how male supremacy hits the ground. Mothers are forced to stay at home, forego an education, give the meat to the men, take the beatings and the rapes, care for the children and the household while working outside the home, care for and raise the children alone, have children for their nation, race, and men. The little girls women bear are groomed to grow into mothers. They are taught this from an early age. Mattel makes a lot of money from their (mis)education. Girls are little mothers, mothers-in-waiting, mothers-to-be. They play with the pink plastic ovens while the boys play with guns. Mothers are cutesy, stupid, dumb, slow, trivial spenders. They buy matching bows and clothes, pick out socks, underwear, bedspreads, and hand towels. Motherhood is dressed up, sold, and made cute and dumb to keep women pretending to be happy thinking they hold a special place in society, as the nurturers of the future, as people with value. It has been said the success of the race, country, or nation depends on the cheerful attitudes of the mothers and their willingness to sacrifice themselves while working for free. Motherhood is sexual servitude.

Motherhood means women exist for men and children. Mothers do not have identities outside of motherhood. They don't need any. They perform their mothering functions and that is why they exist. Period. But a mother's identity rests upon something other than chastity and fresh baked brownies. It rests on what the Christian patriarchs tried so cleverly to cover up when they created the myth of the Virgin Mother, that is, before a woman can become a mother she must be fucked, by a penis or now by medical instruments inserting sperms or embryos. This means that beneath the supposedly esteemed institution of motherhood, there is sex, sin, a fallen woman. Motherhood rests upon whoredom, because to be a mother a woman must have been a whore, have had sex, have sinned. She is Original Sin, Eve incarnate, who tempted Adam with the apple, and like the apple, she must fall before she reproduces. A woman has fallen if she reproduces. Her reproduction is a sign, a mark of her sin. She is in a double bind because to perform her motherly function she must first sin. She then has sexual knowledge; she is used property, ruined. She is sex, a hole, a vagina, a whore. All women are whores is the bottom line, like a sheet pulled cleanly over a corpse, the origin of motherhood is covered up to keep the supposedly esteemed institution of motherhood intact with cute cut-outs of happy cows and what not. Motherhood is the do-all, get-blamed-for-all job that doesn't end, that doesn't get paid, has no insurance, no sick leave, no pension, and no time off. Motherhood puts women in physical danger throughout the pregnancy and during the birth, especially Black women and poor women of all races.[27] Mother must answer to her man. She has little to no power, no money, but is entirely responsible for the outcome of the child. She carries the future child in her body for nine months, a time when the fetus has more personhood rights than she does. She suckles it from her breast (or bottle), is responsible financially for feeding and clothing it because Dad can always leave at any time, if he is there at all. She will lose custody if she stands up to the biological father when he sexually abuses the child even when it is proven that he abuses the child. She gets beaten, especially when she is pregnant,[28] and must promise to stay with the abuser and have more children in order to survive his battering. She is blamed for staying with an abuser, and she is told she is breaking up the family when she leaves him. Her husband prostitutes her. He takes pictures of their sex and sells them. He threatens to show the pictures if she does not do what he wants. She must be an emotional sponge for the child for the rest of her life. Her boychild may physically and verbally abuse her like Dad does or did. She must have the baby when she does not want it because she cannot legally or financially terminate pregnancy or use safe, effective contraception. She is responsible for all contraception, and if she gets pregnant while using contraception she will be told she got pregnant on purpose to trap her man. She can be forced to get an abortion, or be kept from getting an abortion, or be sterilized against her will and without her consent. Her man can keep her from using contraception, exposing her to unwanted pregnancy and diseases. She has to endure medical procedures and drugs designed by male scientists and promoted by multi-national pharmaceutical companies who use her as a guinea pig.[29] The medical procedures are invasive and humiliating. She must succumb to them out of ignorance, lack of viable options, societal pressure, or outright coercion when she attempts to terminate the pregnancy and/or get contraceptive devices installed or shot into her body. In short, no matter how many cute cow knick knacks are produced in poor countries using female labor and marketed in the West, motherhood remains a raw and dangerous deal for the sex subordinate class, woman.

The division between motherhood and whoredom furthers the political effectiveness of male supremacy. It channels women into motherhood and heterosexuality, keeps the respectable women focused on how good they have it (they have homes and are sexually available to one man), how innately chaste they are as compared to the whores who are homeless, dirty, and sexual public property. The division also creates a pool of women and girls who will serve as public fuck pieces. For instance, the raped twelve-year-old is called a whore. She is now ruined property; she is a throw-away. She may run away and prostitute on the streets. Any man can have her, since she is a whore, in the same way that any man can have a wife, but the wife belongs to him alone. A wife is private sexual and reproductive property whereas a whore is public sexual property. The social and political separation of women into the categories of mother and whore prevents any acknowledgment that the rape of the whores happens to all women to one degree or another.

In the 1960s with the advent of sexual liberation liberal men and pimps (often one and the same) supported abortion rights as an issue of privacy because it gave them sexual access to women with very little or no responsibility. It gave them a free fuck and it made them into playboys. Obtaining abortion rights blurred the social line between mother and whore. Now that the fuck does not necessarily lead to pregnancy, marriage, and family, any and every woman can be sexually promiscuous, or sexually exploited as a whore. This made a lot of men happy. The bitches can be banged at will, a doctor can pull it out and then she can be banged some more. It also made a lot of women unhappy, those women who are anti-abortion ostensibly for religious reasons. The church says it is murder. The Pope says it is bad, unnatural, against God's will. Mother Teresa asked, "If a mother can kill her own children, then what can be next?"[30] She cut to the quick of the issue. If abortion is framed as murder, women will not support it. Or women will resort to analyzing abortion as an issue of choice, using terms like pro-choice instead of pro-abortion to soften the ideological blow. Pro-choice ideology and its accompanying terminology fit perfectly in a liberal society, but it does not get to the root of women's oppression. Women's identity relies upon a self-sacrificing motherhood and a nurturing nature. If women do not live up to those ideals they become the bad women, lesbians and whores and other unnatural monsters. Women do not want to kill their own young, women do not do that, whores do that. Women are easily controlled by notions of femininity; if they kill their own children they cannot be mothers, if they are not mothers they are whores, if they are whores their lives are meaningless and marginal and more dangerous than living with one rapist batterer. They lose their supposedly esteemed place in society along with their entire identity. The religious women opposed to abortion know that if abortion is legal it makes them into whores, too. Legal abortion makes it easier for their husbands to fuck around. It makes it easier for their husbands to fuck them, use them for sex and sex only. Religious women do not want to be whores. They want respect, dignity, and meaning. They think they will find it in motherhood. They know they will not find it in whoredom. They are afraid.

Here is where the men step in (again). The religious men play everything they have to feed the fear of their women. It is mom, apple pie, the family, red, white, and blue flags, parades, and overseas war. The religious men stoke their women's moral self-righteousness, a mask the women wear to avoid their fear of being treated as if they are worthless. The religious patriarchs say it is the lesbian feminist women libbers who are going to make the lives of women worse, or who have made the lives of women worse. And the liberal men play their part. They feed the fear of their women. It is anti-sex, anti-men, uptight, and pro-censorship. Liberal men say whoredom is freedom is sexual liberation is groovy, baby. They say those women on the right are outdated frumps and old-fashioned prudes. Be liberated, babe, let us all stick it in you. Now, what feminists know is that neither of these paths is concerned with women's freedom. It is not free to be a mother, breeding and cleaning and caring, nor is it free to be a whore, fucking and fucking and sucking. The reason pimps and liberal men legally support abortion rights as a privacy issue is not because they are such nice guys.[31] It is because it ties in perfectly with male control of women; addressing women's rights as issues of privacy is exactly what men want because they control women, especially in private. Liberal men defend pornography as a matter of privacy. They say it is an individual man's right to use pornography, especially in his home. He expresses his right to free speech when he makes pornography and when he consumes pornography so that the abuse of women equals speech. The man's erection when he watches the abuse of women is also a matter of speech. The erect penis is an act of speech. The rape of the woman in the pornography is speech. The feeling of sexual dominance is speech. The dribbling semen is speech. Now, for everyone who did not know that penises spoke, how all of that equals speech does not make any sense until one thinks about what the u.s. constitution was founded upon: property ownership of land, human beings, and livestock. Then it becomes clear. Under the u.s. constitution, his use of her is the master's use of his property. Rape is merely his expression, as exerted upon his property. The filming and selling of the rape is how he packages his speech. It does not matter that women are hurt to make it and it does not matter that it functions as hate propaganda against women as a class. It does not matter because pornography benefits men politically, socially, and economically and quite simply, men rule.

Male supremacy is changing. It is evolving and this is not a good thing for women. After centuries of reliance upon the institution of marriage and the church to control the female population, male supremacy is now making real the belief that all women are whores. Andrea Dworkin said:

> It used to be marriage and the church that controlled women or that allowed men to control women. They were the institutions of male dominance that mattered along with the legal system. But now those institutions don't have the kind of control over women that they once had. What is happening before your and my very eyes is that the pornography industry has managed to legitimize the sexuality of prostitution and to make it the duty of every woman to perform sexually as a prostitute.[32]

Liberal men have had enough of the illusion of motherhood. A whore in every bedroom and on every street corner is the neo-male supremacist battle cry. The myth of original sin, or the belief that women tempt men to sin (have sex) simply by being women is the crux of misogyny. It has hurt women in the past, it hurts women now, and it will get worse as all women will be increasingly expected to conform to whoredom all of the time. Women are punished when they are whores and they are punished when they are not whores. So, identifying with the label whore or not whore is really a waste of time because both the Christian's hatred of sex and the liberal's supposed love of sex are based on the hatred and degradation of women. Neither way is the path to women's emancipation. Not whore. Not mother. Christian men and liberal men are friendly enemies engaged in a cock fight meant to display their animosity while they fuck women and film the fuck behind the political screen of oppositional politics. Christian men and non-Christian men prostitute and otherwise rape women and girls, in the name of God and in the name of not-God. Male supremacy needs the Left and the Right as two banners for women to rally around looking for male approval, money, and shelter from their respective men. The Left and the Right work together to enslave women. The Left and the Right rape women with impunity while the women spend their time fighting the side they are not on, not realizing that those divisions are blinders, both sides hate them, both sides use them.

Feminists know that in order for women to be emancipated, they must have control of their bodies before sex, during sex, and after sex. Sex and children can never be duties. Abortion must be free and available to all women and girls on demand. The fight for abortion rights is instrumental for women's liberation. Women have to find ways to understand, define, and control abortion on their own terms without state, or religious and liberal men's interference. Given that men stop women from having access to abortion and men force women to abort, men as a class cannot be counted upon to work for the emancipation of women. When men stop women from having access to abortion they violate women's civil rights. When men force their wives or girlfriends to terminate their pregnancies they express the ultimate form of ownership over the mothers and the offspring by destroying the potential child at its point of origin. This is the penis thrust deep into a woman or girl. This is the cesarean section, the probing speculum, and rod used in in-vitro-fertilization. It is the genital mutilation, sewing the girl up tight, the probing fingers and lights and clamps searching to find the status of the hymen. It is the gynecological exam. It is the obsession with the Virgin Mary. It is an attempt to control, own, and master what men deem to be that great void of creation, of life itself found deep inside a woman; explained by science, speculated upon by all the world's religious mythologies, and searched for in outer and inner space. It is what men must know, control, own, categorize, and ultimately destroy for legal, political, social and philosophical domination over women, children, and nature. Over life itself.

Author's note: Dedicated to the memory of my great grandmother, Alvina Stark Hale, who suffered profoundly under male supremacy.

Afterword

Ashley Sovereign

The battlefield for abortion rights has moved from women's bodies to their hearts. Though women today are faced with the threat of clinic terrorism and protester violence, in general the passage of Roe v. Wade has allowed women to have medically safe pregnancy terminations. However, in the current sociopolitical climate any woman finding herself in need of an abortion faces a substantial risk of injury to her dignity and sense of self. Abortion providers and clinic workers are often discouraged by this reality, as they thanklessly strive to provide patients with nonjudgmental, caring, and compassionate services. Unfortunately, despite the frequent success of abortion providers in providing a caring and safe environment, women seeking abortions today do so in an antagonistic cultural environment (with antagonists literally positioned right outside the clinic doors) made up of those who disrespect and judge their choices.

Inside the clinic walls, staff members work to provide women with compassionate affirmations, medically accurate information, and nonjudgmental understanding, but outside of these walls, the increasingly well-funded and well-organized voice of the conservative based "Religious Right" has manipulated, oversimplified, and dichotomized the public discourse. Rather than acknowledging the multiple issues women take into account when deciding about a pregnancy, the Right portrays the decision itself as black and white: women who have abortions are diminished women, and abortion is never a moral choice. Protesters extol a hypocritical version of faith and religion, harshly judging and harassing those who enter the clinic. As someone raised in a family of faith, I see clearly that this physical, emotional, and sexual harassment[33] ignores core principles of religion, such as peace, love, understanding, and compassion. Anti-choice activists disregard these principles in order to accomplish a political objective, while ironically accusing abortion providers and pro-choice individuals of lacking respect for life.

When women were forced to seek illegal abortion services, there was little room for ambivalence in their feelings. Providers, activists, and clergy working in the field since before Roe v. Wade may be unprepared for the ways in which the new strategies employed by the anti's have affected patients. For example, "crisis pregnancy centers" (CPCs) lure women in with false promises of options counseling, abortion information and referrals, and practical assistance, and then provide extensive misinformation about abortion procedures, risks, laws, and availability. Women often leave CPCs unaware of their anti-abortion agenda and mistakenly believe they have received factual medical information. Those of us who work in the abortion field can usually identify women who have been to CPCs by the questions they ask: "When do you cut me open?" "Is the doctor here a *real* doctor?" "Is it true I won't be able to have any children after this?" "Are you going to call my family and tell them what I did?" "Is it true you use the same medical instruments on everyone?" Subsequently, a higher degree of ambivalence and confusion is inevitable, and providers and others concerned with social justice must be informed about how they can best respond to such anti-choice tactics. Nonetheless, one of the greatest testaments to women's determination to end an unwanted pregnancy is that even with these false threats of medical harm ringing in their heads, they have still sought out an abortion.

If women are being injured by their abortion experiences, it is not due to the medical care that health clinics are providing. Rather, it is because a woman must access these services in an environment where she has to endure protesters shouting "murderer" and "whore" while they bizarrely label this harassment "sidewalk counseling." It is because she faces billboards all over town that reduce her personal dilemma and experience to an oversimplified slogan: "Abortion stops a beating heart" "Abortion, a baby can live without it." It is because she must listen to politicians talk about "saving babies" from women who are too confused to make moral decisions. A woman presented with constant images and messages which deride her competency to make a moral choice cannot help but absorb parts of those messages.

Much of the contemporary discourse about abortion is framed in terms of judgment. Both publicly and privately, individuals assess the moral agency of women and speculate upon "their" values and lack of character. How familiar are sentences like these: "She had an abortion for no good reason," or "She's irresponsible," or "I don't believe in abortion when used as birth control." These misogynist statements insinuate that women are inherently selfish, ignorant, and irresponsible and at the least are incapable of managing their lives in a way that is both practically and morally right. It is no wonder that women often characterize themselves as being "against abortion" even when they move heaven and earth to get one. They are attempting to separate themselves from the public image of women who have abortions, an image created and managed by the Right.

Anti-choice agendas often are disguised as "pro-family" or "pro-adoption" messages. The right wing has manipulatively co-opted the language and spirit of feminism, which has led to increased confusion among the public. For example, there are networks of anti-abortion groups that regard women who have chosen abortions as "victims" and use the language of the battered women's movement to pathologize normal emotional responses to termination as "post-traumatic stress disorder." There is also the expansion of legislation that personifies the fetus, supposedly to increase punishment against those who injure a fetus while battering a woman. Though this so-called fetal rights legislation is nominally trying to protect women from harm (and increase accountability of those who inflict harm on pregnant women), in reality these measures are designed to criminalize abortion.

Abortion is also a class and race issue. The most marginalized women (low-income, rural, teenage, or women of color) are disproportionately impacted by restrictions put on abortion. When the Right Wing attempts to pass "waiting period" laws that purport to protect women from themselves, women without adequate resources are most negatively affected. Because of these so-called waiting periods, women without paid leave—primarily low-income women—are forced to take off additional time from work, which means less money for their families. Women living in isolated rural communities are required to pay for lodging and extra expenses for travel, and teens are forced to miss additional school. Because there are so few abortion providers left, clinics report that some patients, who travel long distances and are unable to afford lodging, sleep in the clinic parking lot. It is not difficult to imagine how government-imposed "waiting periods" additionally complicate their lives. One would think that if the Right Wing were truly as "pro-family" as they contend, rather than create additional barriers to women who are trying to take care of themselves and their families, they would stop chipping away at what little public assistance is left for the working poor.

The anti-choice factions will inevitably suggest adoption as the *deus ex machina* answer to each woman's problem of unintended pregnancy. One reason this is not always acceptable is that pregnant women will often reject adoption for many of the same reasons they reject parenting—because both choices involve the significantly unpredictable, laborious, potentially risky and damaging process of gestation and delivery. Anti-choice groups seldom address the painful emotions and grief that come with relinquishing a child, or the fact that she might lose her job or be kicked out of her home if her pregnancy is discovered. If a woman is unable or unwilling to put her body, heart, mind, and spirit through a pregnancy, abortion is the only option available to her.

Another problem with adoption is that the system is subject to the same social problems and biases that affect the rest of the world. Sadly, older children, children of color, children of drug addicted parents, children with disabilities, or those with other "undesirable" characteristics are unlikely to be sought after by prospective parents. In addition, restrictions on who can adopt a child (unmarried individuals, those who have been charged with minor criminal offenses, and so on) and the expenses involved in adopting a child, can be prohibitive. The result is that many children wait in temporary foster placements for parents that will never appear.

Other well-meaning individuals, on either side of the abortion debate, will recommend better use of birth control as a route to reduce the need for abortion. Though birth control education needs to be improved, this is not a simple solution either. Those who chastise women for using abortion as birth control need to realize the boundaries of available and accessible contraception. Methods for preventing pregnancy are limited, and women have legitimate reasons for rejecting one method or another. Contraceptive hormone methods may be relatively effective, but they carry risks including stroke, high blood pressure, and blood clots. Spermicides often cause irritation and infection, and are famously undependable. IUDs are not recommended for women who have not yet had children, or whose partners may not be monogamous. And in order to use condoms effectively, women must depend on their male partners, who have less at stake in avoiding a pregnancy. Finally, it must not be overlooked that women frequently use birth control methods, and these methods often fail. Absolutely nothing, including sterilization or planned abstinence, is one hundred percent effective. The issue of birth control must be understood within a larger societal context: it is no accident that there are minimal research dollars allocated for an effective male birth control pill or that federal health plans reject contraceptive coverage yet provide coverage for impotence treatment.

The answers to complex social problems are never simple, and abortion is no exception. However, it is clear that we must examine the assumptions inherent in the language used to discuss pregnancy and women's reproductive health options. When even staunchly pro-choice activists use the lexicon of "forgiveness" when talking about abortion, we perpetuate a discourse that minimizes and disrespects the responsibilities women must take into account when negotiating through a lifetime of fertility decisions. As pro-choice activists and individuals concerned about women, their partners and their children, we must develop new ways to talk about abortion and develop strategies that do not capitulate to the manipulations and shaming voices of the Right Wing.

About the Editor

Krista Jacob is founder and editor of the online journal *Sexing the Political: A Journal of Third Wave Feminists on Sexuality*, located at www.sexingthepolitical.com. She has a long history of involvement in women's issues, which includes working as a victim advocate for rape and domestic violence survivors for ten years and as an abortion counselor for four years. At present, she is a writer, mother, and is an on-call Reproductive Health Counselor.

Ms. Jacob received her Bachelor's degree from the University of Iowa, and her Master of Science in Women's Studies from Minnesota State University, Mankato. She currently lives in the Midwest with her husband Jim, and their son Maxwell.

Notes

FOREWORD
[1]. Henshaw, S. K. 1998a. "Unintended pregnancy in the United States." *Family Planning Perspectives* 30:24-29 & 46.
[2]. Koonin, L. M. et al. 2000. "Abortion surveillance-United States, 1997." *CDC Surveillance Summaries*. December 8. MMWR 2000; 49 (no. SS-11):1-43.

INTRODUCTION
[3]. Angela Bonavoglia, *The Choices We Made: Twenty-five Women and Men Speak Out about Abortion*. (New York: Random House, 1991),122.
[4]. Christiane Northrup, *Women's Bodies, Women's Wisdom: Creating Physical and Emotional Health and Healing*. (New York: Bantam Books, 1998), 385.
[5]. "Abortion experience" is meant to encompass the entire process women go through when ending a pregnancy. It includes each step of their choice, from the discovery of the pregnancy (or fetal problems) to any experiences and feelings subsequent to the abortion procedure.

PART I: ABORTION TESTIMONIES: BEFORE AND AFTER LEGAL ABORTION
[6]. I found these women thanks to teachers who made announcements in class about my project. And they found me; they had never told their story from start to finish and needed to. The interview process is a nerve-wracking one, but somewhere in the middle of each interview we didn't feel like strangers anymore, and it stopped being an interview and became an emotional exchange. I kept the format of my interviews as simple as possible. My questions were: 1) Under what circumstances did you get, and find out that you were pregnant? 2) What factors influenced your decision to abort? 3) Do you feel your decision was supported by those you told? 4) What was the actual procedure like for you, emotionally and physically? 5) How did you feel afterward and now about your decision, yourself, etc.?

7. Audre Lorde, *Sister Outsider: Essays & Speeches by Audre Lorde* (Freedom, California: The Crossing Press Feminist Series, 1984), 41. This essay was originally a paper delivered at the Modern Language Association's "Lesbian and Literature Panel," Chicago, Illinois, December 28, 1977. First published in *Sinister Wisdom 6* (1978) and *The Cancer Journals* (San Francisco: Spinsters, Ink, 1980).

8. Carol Gilligan, *In A Different Voice: Psychological Theory and Women's Development* (Cambridge, MA: Harvard University Press, 1993), 74-75. This piece is inspired by a conversation I had with a Catholic patient in 1993; as women, even if we are adamantly pro-choice, rarely do we tell our "abortion stories."

9. There are many people who helped to create a positive atmosphere in a situation so foreign to me. Some of you know how much I appreciate the part you played in my spiritual journey. For others, my gratitude has been implied but never spoken. My sincere thanks to: 1) My co-workers in the clinic who supported me from beginning to end without any judgement. 2) The doctor who performed the abortion; she is an amazing woman. I see her from time to time in the clinic, and I am sure my face blends in with the thousands of other women she has helped over the years. But I always feel personally connected to her. I want her to know how much her compassionate care meant to me. 3) My partner who accompanied me on this journey, and encouraged me to move through my feelings, even though it scared him. 4) The being that touched my life and changed it in many ways. Sometimes I wonder if you would have had his eyes and my smile, but I accept that for every road I choose, there is another I leave behind. I honor your message by remaining open to the possibilities you provided me.

PART II: VOICES FROM INSIDE THE ABORTION CLINIC

10. The photographs in this series are reprinted with the permission of DeDe VanSlyke and the Midwest Health Center for Women. They are not to be reprinted, for any reason, without the written permission of DeDe VanSlyke, and Midwest Health Center for Women.

11. Physicians for Reproductive Choice and Health state that "less than 1% of the 40,000 practicing OB/GYNs in the United States offer abortion services." For more information, please visit Medical Students for Choice www.ms4c.org and Physicians for Reproductive Choice and Health www.prch.org

PART III: ORGANIZING FOR CHANGE: RELIGIOUS AND POLITICAL ACTIVISTS SPEAK OUT

12. "Incidents of Violence and Disruption Against Abortion Providers-1977-2002," as of 1/31/02 National Abortion Federation, www.prochoice.org.
13. Deborah Walsh, personal correspondence, Feb. 1998.
14. Renee Chelian, prepared editorial comments released on January 22, 1998.
15. "Unintended Pregnancies in US," Henshaw, Stanley, *Family Planning Perspectives* v. 330 #1 Jan/Feb. 1998.
16. *Pregnant? Need Help? Pregnancy Options Workbook* Ferre Institute, 124 Front St., Binghamton NY 13905 single copy $3.50 postpaid or at www.pregnancyoptions.info
17. National Association of Abortion Funds www.nnaf.org.
18. For other views on the state of the abortion issue, see www.ncap.com, the National Coalition of Abortion Providers.
19. Mrs. Sally Kauer spent many years working with the Midland Coalition for Choice. She acted as the main go-between between the women and girls we helped and the women' health clinics. She was proud to be a member of Planned Parenthood. A mother of three adult children, Sally was a well-known pianist, choir director, and church organist and also known in the area for her wonderful dahlias. She died in December of 2000.
20. *Reproductive Freedom News* (v.vii.n.1)).
21. Myth is a powerful creator of and justification for political and social reality, so that the various dominant mythologies, religious, political, and social are believed to be real, right, and true, based upon nature or God or science. They are the status quo and any challenge to them is viewed as an attack against the dominant class.
22. *Eunuchs for the Kingdom of Heaven*; Uta Ranke-Heinemann; Page 31.
23. "Hillary blames conflict between Clinton's grandmother and mother for his sexual infidelities," *The Sunday Oregonian*, August 8, 1999 Page A2. Rapist's mothers are often accused of having done something to make their sons into rapists. Before the Boston Strangler was apprehended a profile speculated that he killed because he was consumed by mother hatred. In fact he loved his mother, it was his father who was cruel and abusive.

[24]. Like pop culture's answer to high brow art, porn stores sell plastic woman parts such as blow-up dolls and plastic vaginas while the more serious woman parts such as womb machines are found in universities, hospitals, and other research labs.

[25]. Men take out rape hits on their girlfriends or ex-wives. For instance, a man made public his girlfriend's home address on the Internet along with a note saying she liked rough sex and wanted to be raped. Six men showed up at her house. A website called the "Nuremburg Trial" called for abortion doctors to be killed.

[26]. Using the term abnormal to describe women in relation to men is originally Marilyn Frye's idea.

[27]. Black women are "three times more likely to die from complications of pregnancy and childbirth." *Killing the Black Body*, by Dorothy Roberts, p. 234.

[28]. The increase in battering against women during pregnancy is well documented. Please see: Guard, A. (1997). *Violence and teen pregnancy: A resource guide for MCH practitioners.* Newton, MA: Children's Safety Network, EDC, Inc.; and Musick, J. (1993). *Young, poor, and pregnant: The psychology of teen motherhood.* New Haven, CT: Yale University Press.

[29]. For example, American Home Products makes and markets fen-phen and Norplant contraceptive implants. Thousands of women who were damaged by fen-phen and Norplant have filed suit against the pharmaceutical company. *The Oregonian*, Saturday, August 7, 1999. Page A1.

[30]. *Whatever Happened to the Human Race?* C. Everett Koop and Francis Schaeffer. Crossway Books.

[31]. *Playboy* has sponsored pro-choice work, in an attempt to buy off feminists and entrench the political likeness of abortion and pornography as non-gendered privacy issues.

[32]. Andrea Dworkin, from a speech given at the University of Minnesota in 1998 co-sponsored by the Minnesota Coalition Against Prostitution and the Program Against Sexual Violence.

AFTERWORD

[33]. Unbelievably, I have observed protesters harass patients and clinic staff by asking if they become sexually aroused by the vacuum aspirator.

BIBLIOGRAPHY

Bonavoglia, Angela. *The Choices We Made: Twenty-five Women and Men Speak Out About Abortion.* New York: Random House, 1991.

Everett Koop, C. and Schaeffer, Francis A. *Whatever Happened to the Human Race?* Illinois: Crossway Books, 1979.

Gilligan, Carol. *In A Different Voice: Psychological Theory and Women's Development.* Cambridge, MA: Harvard University Press, 1993.

Henshaw, SK. "Unintended pregnancy in the United States." Family Planning Perspectives 30:24-29 & 46, 1998a.

Koonin LM et al. "Abortion surveillance-United States, 1997." CDC Surveillance Summaries, December 8. MMWR 2000;49 (no. SS-11):1-43.

Lorde, Audre. *Sister Outsider: Essays & Speeches by Audre Lorde.* Freedom, California; The Crossing Press, 1984.

Northrup, Christiane M.D. *Women's Bodies, Women's Wisdom: Creating Physical and Emotional Health and Healing.* New York: Bantam Books, 1998.

Ranke-Heinemann, Uta. *Eunuchs for the Kingdom of Heaven: Women, Sexuality, and the Catholic Church.* New York: Doubleday, 1990.

Roberts, Dorothy. *Killing the Black Body.* New York: Vintage Books, 1999.

Welch, Sharon. *A Feminist Ethic of Risk.* Minneapolis: Fortress Press, 1990.

0-595-23001-6